P9-DMG-834

WHEN GOD WINKS AT YOU

How God Speaks Directly to You
Through the Power of Coincidence

BY SQUIRE RUSHNELL

THOMAS NELSON
Since 1798

NASHVILLE   DALLAS   MEXICO CITY   RIO DE JANEIRO   BEIJING

Published in Nashville, Tennessee, by Thomas Nelson. Thomas Nelson is a registered trademark of Thomas Nelson, Inc.

Thomas Nelson, Inc., titles may be purchased in bulk for educational, business, fund-raising, or sales promotional use. For information, please e-mail SpecialMarkets@ThomasNelson.com.

Scripture quotations marked NKJV are taken from the NEW KING JAMES VERSION®. © 1982 by Thomas Nelson, Inc. Used by permission. All rights reserved.

Scripture quotations marked NCV are taken from the NEW CENTURY VERSION®. © 2005 by Thomas Nelson, Inc. Used by permission. All rights reserved.

Scripture quotations marked NIV are from the *Holy Bible*, NEW INTERNATIONAL VERSION®. © 1973, 1978, 1984 by International Bible Society. Used by permission of Zondervan Publishing House. All rights reserved.

Scripture quotations noted KJV are from the *Holy Bible*, KING JAMES VERSION.

Scripture quotations noted NLT are from the *Holy Bible*, NEW LIVING TRANSLATION, © 1996. Used by permission of Tyndale House Publishers, Inc., Wheaton, Illinois 60189. All rights reserved.

Scripture quotations marked CEV are from THE CONTEMPORARY ENGLISH VERSION of the Bible, © 1991, 1995 by the American Bible Society. Used by permission.

Scripture quotations marked The Message are taken from The Message by Eugene H. Peterson, © 1993, 1994, 1995, 1996, 2000, 2001, 2002. Used by permission of NavPress Publishing Group. All rights reserved.

Library of Congress Cataloging-in-Publication Data

Rushnell, SQuire D., 1938–
    When God winks at you: how God speaks directly to you through the power of coincidence / SQuire Rushnell.
      p. cm.
    Includes bibliographical references (p.233).
    ISBN 978-0-7852-1892-0 (hardcover)
    ISBN 978-0-7852-8967-8 (SE)
    1. Coincidence—Religious aspects—Christianity. 2. Christian life.
I. Title.
BV4599.5.C65R87 2006
231.7—dc22
2006009943

Printed in the United States of America

19 20 LSC 38 37 36 35

⠿ ⠿ ⠿ CONTENTS

CONTENTS

CHAPTER ONE

GODWINKS ARE PERSONAL

You've had another one of those days. Everything seems uncertain.

You think: *Wouldn't it be great to wake up one morning and have everything certain?* Certain in love? Certain about your job? Certain about your future?

Who could you talk to about this? Bigger question, who'd listen?

Tentatively your eyes drift skyward.

Hello? Are You there, God?

Then your mind quickly assesses the immensity of your request. You want God to listen to *you*, right now. How ridiculous. There are six billion people on this planet. What if they're all calling God at the same time?

You slump. Deeper into the dumps.

Then—something happens.

A silly little thing.

Someone you just thought about for the first time in years, telephones out of the blue—a silly little coincidence, so silly you shrug it off. Or a prayer you didn't really expect to be answered—was! Immediately, your left brain repeats something you once heard: *There's a mathematical explanation for everything.*

"But . . ." you say, "mayyyyybe . . . it's *not* just coincidence or chance!"

Maybe God *is* communicating with you.

Yes, directly to *you!*

You shake your head.

Naw. Couldn't be.

But . . . what if God *is* communicating with you—in a nonverbal way—making a little miracle happen, right in front of you? After all, God doesn't speak to people in a human voice. He's God . . . He'd do something no one else could do, just to show you it's *Him!*

If so, that would mean that He *is* listening! Right?

He *has* heard you!

What if through this odd little coincidence, or answered prayer, He's sending you—*you* . . . out of all those billions of people—a direct, *personal* message of reassurance? To stop worrying? To keep the faith? That everything will be all right?

This, my dear reader, is the essence of this book.

THIS BOOK IS ABOUT YOU

Every time you receive what some call a coincidence or an answered prayer, it's a direct and personal message of reassurance from God to you—what I call a *godwink*.

It's similar to when you were a kid sitting at the dining room table. You looked up and saw someone you loved looking back. Mom or Dad or Granddad. They gave you a little wink.

You had a nice feeling from that small silent communication.

What did it mean? Probably—"Hey kid . . . I'm thinking about you right this moment. I'm proud of you. Everything is going to be all right."

That's what a godwink is.

Every so-called coincidence or answered prayer is God's way of giving you *His* small, silent communication. A little wink saying, "Hey kid! I'm thinking of *you* . . . right now!"

> The LORD your God has chosen you out of all the peoples on the face of the earth to be . . . his treasured possession.
>
> —DEUTERONOMY 7:6 NIV

It's a clear message of reassurance—that no matter how uncertain your life seems at the moment, He *will* help move you toward certainty.

And it's a sign that you're never alone. In fact, you're always on His GPS—a global positioning system I like to call God's Positioning System.

In this book I aim to show that every godwink that happens in your life is a very personal experience. I've collected one compelling story after another to convince you that you will never again have to wonder where you rank among those six billion others in this world. Like those in the stories that follow, the instant you receive a godwink, you'll know it. You are right there at the top.

WHEN IT'S CRYSTAL CLEAR

In Anaheim, California, Mavis Jackson drove past the Crystal Cathedral. For twenty years, she said the same thing: "Someday I'm going to go there."

One Sunday morning, she did. Putting on her best outfit, she simply decided, "Today is the day."

Getting there early, Mavis took a seat in the middle and watched the huge three-thousand-seat megachurch fill with people. She was awed as the majestic voices of the choir seemed to encircle her. She marveled at the manner in which a huge section of the glass ceiling slid open at the start of the service as if to invite even the birds to worship.

At the end of the service, Mavis stood up and waited for the aisle to clear. Trying not to sound too excited, she said to the young lady who'd been next to her, "I am so glad I came today. Wasn't it wonderful?"

The young woman nodded.

"Are you from here?" asked Mavis.

"No, I'm from the Midwest," said the young woman, adding, "I'm actually here on a mission. To find my birth mother."

There was a pause.

"I know how you must feel," said Mavis. "A long time ago, I had to give up a little girl for adoption. I didn't want to . . . but . . ."

Another pause.

The young woman looked deeply into Mavis's eyes.

"Do you . . . remember her birthday?"

"Yes," said Mavis cautiously. "October 30th."

"That's *my* birthday," gasped the young woman.

That's right! A remarkable "coincidence"—a godwink—had reunited a long lost mother and daughter. What are the odds of that?

They sat down.

The young woman introduced herself as Cheryl Wallace.

Cheryl explained that for years she had been haunted by the lingering uncertainty of not knowing who her birth mother was and, more important, why her mother had given her up.

In her small Midwest town, everyone was discouraging. "You're looking for a needle in a haystack," counseled the town clerk.

"There's no trace of her," said others.

> In his heart a man plans his course, but the Lord determines his steps.
> —PROVERBS 16:9 NIV

Eventually, a suggestion from someone who thought she'd once heard that Cheryl's birth mother had moved to Orange County, California, led her to this time and place.

Even on her most optimistic days, Cheryl *never* could have forecast such a remarkable outcome—that such uncertainty would end with such certainty, in a manner that only God could have made happen.

And when they confirmed that their wonderful miracle was true—that they were long lost mother and daughter—they knew that Mother's Day would never be the same again.

:: :: ::

What can you learn from Mavis and Cheryl's stories? That a mighty force is out there, bigger than all of us, watching over us, directing our lives. And when we step out in faith, as demonstrated by Cheryl in looking for her mother, we *can* receive the desires of our heart. We can turn uncertainty into certainty.

I wonder if, in your past, you were challenged to step out in faith . . . perhaps at an early age. And, as a result, you were given a firm affirmation that your faith would be rewarded. If so, perhaps your experience parallels the one that follows.

TIM'S AMAZING STORY

"When you grow up in a place like Chagrin Falls, Ohio," says world famous comedian Tim Conway, "it's a religious experience in itself. Everyone in town cares for you . . . watches out for you."

Tim Conway's hometown personified Norman Rockwell normalcy. Between Sunday services at the community's two churches, the town folk, like a huge family, involved themselves in each other's lives. Doctors left home each morning to mend hurts, mechanics to fix people's cars, and teachers to grow the minds of children while little girls hopscotched on chalk-etched sidewalks and boys balanced bamboo fishing poles as they made their way to the river bank.

At the age of twelve, Tim had a paper route, tasted chewing gum from the bottom of a chair, and wished he could own a Red Ryder BB gun.

God was a large, mysterious presence in the boy's life. Even though he had no proof that God existed, everybody said He did, and there was no reason to doubt them.

Also looming large in the mind of the Chagrin Falls boy was the annual Blossom Festival, highlighted by the biggest parade of the year and the arrival of the carnival.

Down by the river, a magical mini-village sprang up overnight. A giant Ferris wheel stretched higher than the church tower, the repetitive song of the merry-go-round filled the air, and the fragrance of popcorn and axle grease reached his nostrils.

Fifty cents jangled in Tim's pocket as he made his way to the midway after Saturday chores. He liked the feel of turning the dimes in his pocket.

After drinking a Coke and buying a ticket for the Ferris

wheel, he carefully conducted a survey of the game booths, ascertaining which might secure him the best prize.

Then he saw it! A white plastic crucifix that glowed in the dark, hanging on a green ribbon. For some unknown reason, its lure was powerful.

A man with long hair and dirty fingernails announced that for a mere ten cents, Tim could surely win a nice prize . . . maybe even the one he was eyeing. Grasping the fishing pole, Tim waved the line and hook above the small pool of water where sixty plastic ducks bobbled, some designating a prize but only one entitling its captor to the crucifix that glowed in the dark.

First dime, first try. Nothing.

Second dime, second try . . . he hooked a plastic duck. But only a cheap charm was his reward.

Third dime, last try. One more worthless item.

With each failure, the degree of difficulty became more apparent, and the crucifix more desirable. But he was out of money.

Tim began walking back home, thinking about how good that cross would have looked, glowing in the dark, in his room at night.

Slumping head down, pondering his plight, Tim wished he could have had it.

Darn it.

That instant he spotted the treasure . . . a shiny dime . . . lying on the sidewalk. Reaching down in what retrospectively seemed like slow motion, Tim lifted that dime and broke into a trot back to the midway.

> Delight yourself also in the Lord, And He shall give you the desires of your heart.
> —Psalm 37:4 NKJV

Again he surveyed the situation. One chance in sixty to rescue that glow-in-the-dark crucifix from those murky waters. With his hand in his pocket, he rolled the dime in his fingers just to be sure it was still there. But this was too big a moment. This required big attention.

He left the midway.

Against the trunk of a large maple tree, Tim placed his head on his arm and decided to test the mysterious power of God.

"Lord . . . " he hesitated, unsure of the proper words to speak to the Almighty, "I would . . . really like . . . that white cross. The one . . . on the green ribbon . . . that glows in the dark."

Tim turned from the tree and walked firmly to the carnival booth. Now familiar with him, the man with the long hair and dirty fingernails looked down at Tim, slightly raised an eyebrow, and stretched out his grimy palm.

The dime emerged from Tim's pocket and was quickly parted from him.

The man handed him the pole.

Tim furrowed his brow, pursed his lips just enough for the tip of his tongue to stick out, steadied the pole above the water, and with the concentration of a major league pitcher, he dipped the hook . . . and snatched the number-one duck from the odds of the impossible—awarding him the glow-in-the-dark white crucifix on a green ribbon!

"I kept that cross under my pillow until I went to college," says Tim. "I still have it."

Through many subsequent years, each containing chapters of uncertainty—from college exams to casting calls—Tim Conway was always bolstered by the assurance he'd gained that day, next to a maple tree at the carnival in Chagrin Falls. A small trinket was his enduring confirmation that he'd had a personal answer to his prayer—a godwink he'd never forget.

TEST

How about you? Does it seem, like it did to Tim Conway, that God is a mysterious, intangible entity? People *say* He exists, but you're not quite sure?

Why don't you test Him?

Try putting your total trust in His existence, as Tim did, and just see if you, too, receive a direct, personal communication by way of a wink.

WHEN GOD SMILES

Danielle loved smiley faces. She'd stick them up around her room. Send them in greeting cards. Draw them on correspondence—a round face with two eyes and a smile.

"They matched her personality," said her father, Daniel Heard.

A musically gifted nearly nineteen-year-old, she was about to journey to Los Angeles from her home in Michigan to meet with record producers who thought her songs—she'd composed more than twenty—might have commercial appeal.

Then the tragedy happened. A car out of control. A head-on collision. She died.

We simply cannot fathom the pain borne by her grieving parents and Danielle's two older sisters. Life does not prepare us for that kind of heartbreak.

Nine months later, her father was still feeling agonizing

loss. Daniel stood alone on the rear deck of their home, look-ing off into the woods. It was a dark night. Black clouds filled the sky.

"Oh God . . . this still hurts. Dear God . . . please give me a sign that Danielle is okay. That she's with you," he wailed. Then bowing his head, his voice cracking with sorrow, he said, "I guess I'm not worthy."

A glimmer of light reflected from the deck. He looked up to see a wondrous sight—a hole had formed in the blackness of the sky, just enough for the full moon to fit perfectly into it. He stared, recognizing the craters near the top that looked like the eyes of the man in the moon. Then in slow motion, across the bottom of the moon, a narrow dark cloud drifted . . . and stopped . . . and turned up its corners.

In a direct, personal communication, Daniel was receiving a godwink.

For a full fifteen or twenty seconds, the full moon was a per-fect smiley face, just like those Danielle had always collected.

"I now counsel other parents who are dealing with grief," said Daniel. "I tell them they should expect that their hurt, anger, and sorrow will come in waves. Some days they will be fine. Other days, months later, they'll break down in tears. And occasionally, they'll get a sign—a godwink—to lift their spirits."

Three months after he witnessed the smiley face in the sky,

Daniel and his wife, Paula, moved into their new home. For one year, it had been under construction, positioned on the five-acre lot Danielle had suggested before her accident.

It was a cold Sunday afternoon. Daniel knew that before first snowfall he had to pick up all the scraps of wood and debris left by the electricians, contractors, and siding men. For three hours he labored, pushing a heavy wheelbarrow with loads of debris over the muddy terrain. All the while, Danielle was not far from his mind. Over and over again, he thought about the smiley-faced moon. He was glad God had spoken to him. He now knew Danielle was okay, but . . . he wanted to know that she was *with* Him.

His eyes moistened. A constriction grew in his throat. Out loud, all alone, he cried.

For another few minutes, Daniel labored, satisfied the job was just about finished. He stood, looked around to see if there were any more scraps of wood.

> Weeping may endure for a night, But joy comes in the morning.
>
> —Psalm 30:5 NKJV

There . . . there was one. He went to it and squatted to pick it up. It was a piece of siding, maybe ten inches long. He lifted it, turned it over. His eyes widened. Carved into the wood, probably by a nail, were the words:

"Hi, Dad."

For several moments of disbelief and absolute wonder, he stared at the godwink he held in his hands!

He couldn't wait to get inside to share the story with his wife, Paula. They talked about it. About the significance of the smiley-faced moon and the scrap of siding, both coming within moments of a plea to God for a sign of assurance that their daughter was in heaven.

Paula noted that the siding man worked with his son. Probably that's how those words "Hi, Dad" got there. Then they looked at each other and simultaneously shrugged: "So what?" Whoever left that scrap of wood was a Godwink Link.

GODWINK LINKS

God uses others as unwitting messengers of godwinks to each of us. In fact, we *all* become deliverers of goodness to others without the slightest clue that God is using us that way.

When someone we're thinking about telephones out of the blue, we almost never stop to ask what *caused* that person to call at that very moment. Or when someone you encounter changes the whole course of your life—you usually don't ask why that person was at that place at that moment.

They were Godwink Links.

:: :: ::

In the preceding story, the important thing was not *who* the messenger was, but that a small scrap of wood—the last one Daniel was to pick up—carried the very personal message that God had orchestrated for him to receive.

Think about the times that *you* were the link—the person who happened to call out of the blue just as someone was thinking about you—or you just happened to encounter someone, the result of which was an alteration to the course of *their* life. You were the Godwink Link . . . the unwitting messenger of God's goodness.

Now that I've drawn your attention to it . . . feels good, doesn't it?

THE PICTURE

"I didn't know you were royalty," Janet's friend had scrawled facetiously across the photo in the *New York Daily Mirror*. "She looks just like you."

Janet smiled.

True. The picture of the woman getting a divorce from a

British marquess did look like her—dark hair, worn shoulder length. Janet was amused, and she tucked away the newspaper clipping, dated May 21, 1954, with some of her other memorabilia.

Fifty years passed.

At age thirty-eight, David Gutterman had come to that place in life where he'd accepted the notion that if the right girl didn't happen along, he'd tolerate staying single. But when he met Romaine Orthwein, a thirty-nine-year-old fine art photographer, he knew she was the one. And she felt the same way. They'd met on a blind date, and there was an instant attraction.

In a rapidly moving courtship, David and Romaine visited the home of his parents in Westchester County, New York. Spotting a collection of framed family photos, Romaine was astonished.

"Your mother looks just like my mother did," she said pensively, thinking of the image of her own mom in a photo on her bureau. Romaine's mom had died when Romaine was only nine years old.

"That was my mom's engagement picture," remarked David as they continued their tour of the house.

Over the next few months, David and Romaine's chemistry continued to click, and soon they were talking about marriage. David began thinking how he could make the proposal special.

Then it dawned on him. On several occasions, Romaine had suggested they leave Brooklyn where they lived and go into Manhattan to visit some SoHo art galleries. Frankly, he'd been unenthusiastic about that notion but, perhaps now, this could be the perfect ploy to get her alone in a place she'd never forget.

"It's such a nice day, why don't we walk across the Brooklyn Bridge, then grab a cab on the other side into SoHo?" he suggested nonchalantly.

Romaine was thrilled.

Halfway across the bridge, David motioned for them to stop and sit on a bench. This was the moment he'd planned.

"I have a present for you," he said, pulling a wrapped gift the size of a book from his pocket.

"Oh, I love presents!" exclaimed Romaine, thinking it might be a book of poetry.

Inside was a silver frame with a striking photograph of the two of them that she'd never seen. In the picture they were dancing, David was whispering something into Romaine's ear, and she was smiling.

"Thank you so much. I love it!" said Romaine.

"How do you like the frame?" asked David.

She looked at him quizzically.

"It's silver," he prompted. "It matches the box."

"What box?"

From his other pocket he pulled an antique silver ring box. It was engraved with Romaine's name. Inside was the ring.

"Will you marry me?" he asked as she opened the box.

Sparkles in her eyes, she smiled, hugged him, and said, "Yes. Oh yes!"

They ran all the way back to Brooklyn to make phone calls to tell everyone.

"I knew he didn't really want to go to those art galleries," said Romaine playfully.

In a quiet moment, cupping the antique silver ring box in her hands, she wistfully thought of her mother—wishing she could be with her now to share her joy.

Preparations for the wedding began immediately. Romaine scheduled an engagement party in St. Louis, where her father lived and she grew up, and another one in New York where David was raised.

Just before the first engagement party in St. Louis, David's mother, Janet Gutterman, called to apologize that she was unable to attend. She was feeling ill.

"I really wanted Romaine's family to meet you . . . " said David with a note of disappointment.

"Well . . . why don't you just take a picture of me?" she replied good-heartedly, trying to make the best of an unfortunate situation.

"Is that a good idea?" joked David in return. "I mean, if you look so much like Romaine's mother, wouldn't that startle her father?"

"Tell me more about Romaine's mother," inquired Janet with interest, mentally noting that David had previously mentioned their similar looks.

"Well, she was married to the Marquess of Milford-Haven, David Mountbatten. Then she married Romaine's father about ten years before she died," he said, testing his memory.

That triggered a thought.

Why does that feel familiar? wondered Janet—something from long ago.

Later, nagged by curiosity, she went to a small trunk in the attic where she kept memorabilia. Sifting through souvenirs of past years, she came upon the old newspaper clipping that, for some reason, she had kept. The 1954 photo of a woman whose likeness of her appeared in the *New York Daily Mirror*, the one a friend had sent with the note "She looks just like you."

As Janet glanced at the caption on the old photo, she gasped. She immediately called her son. "David, I have an old picture in a newspaper . . . I can't believe it," she said breathlessly. "I have goose bumps! The woman who looks like me in the newspaper . . . *is* Romaine's mother!"

She reread the caption just to be sure it was true. It had to be—Romaine had said that she and her mother shared the same first name. The caption on the old newspaper photo stated that Romaine Pierce Simpson was divorcing the Marquess of Milford-Haven.

"I was speechless," said David. "A photo that appeared in a newspaper long before Romaine or I were even born, reemerged fifty years to the month, May 2004, just as we were planning our engagement party. What are the chances of that? And that our mothers would look exactly alike, with the same facial features, wearing their hair identically?"

> For the truly faithful, no miracle is necessary. For those who doubt, no miracle is sufficient.[1]
> —NANCY GIBBS

"Then, think about this," he continued. "My wife and her mother were both named Romaine . . . and both were married to a man named David. Two Romaines and two Davids."

"I was shocked," said Romaine. "I'm no stranger to coincidence . . . I believe coincidence happens for a reason. But I was blown away. I felt that my mother was communicating her tremendous approval of David."

Today a picture of Romaine's mother still sits on her bureau, facing the picture of David and her smiling and dancing—next to the engraved silver ring box.

In Janet Gutterman's scrapbook, there are side-by-side photos of two mothers, nearly identical.

GOD *IS*

In broken English, the older man spoke hesitantly from the pulpit, uncertain that his audience would comprehend his sermon.

His son, Arthur Caliandro, beamed from the congregation of his peers at the prestigious Union Theological Seminary in New York.

One of the cherished honors of senior classmen with a father in the ministry was to have him invited to speak. Arthur knew that his father had nervously anticipated this day. A native of Italy, he had migrated to Portland, Maine, where he became the respected pastor of a small Italian-American church. But today, preaching in this bastion of theological study, he only hoped that despite his Italian accent, he could make his son proud.

Arthur's father had developed an engaging manner of using illustrations to underscore his message. On this morning, he told a story that exemplified how God sometimes uses mysterious means to personally and directly communicate with us. It was the story of a man from the Midwest who had become startled when a gust of wind from an open window toppled a picture frame on his bedroom bureau. It was a photo of the man's father. Only later did he learn that at that precise moment, his father had died.

Arthur was mortified.

With an air of youthful arrogance, he worried what his classmates would think of such an unsophisticated story.

"Daddy! Why did you use that story?" he later snapped at his father.

Instantly he knew his words stung. They had pierced his father's heart . . . and hurt his feelings. For many years thereafter, Arthur wished that he could have recaptured his careless comment—hoping that his father *truly* knew that he *had* been proud of him on that day long ago.

Years passed.

Arthur Caliandro unfurled an impressive career in the ministry, and for more than two decades, he has been a powerful communicator from the pulpit of the famed Marble Collegiate Church in New York City as the handpicked successor of Dr. Norman Vincent Peale.

One summer, Arthur and his family were vacationing on a small island off the coast of Maine. His younger brother was there with his wife and children, as well as the wife and children of his older brother Bruno, who had remained in New

York. Their days were filled with disparate activities—gabbing grown-ups and youngsters in motion.

Late one morning, an island breeze carried the shrill whistle of the fire station.

Bruno's wife, Carol, in an uncharacteristic gesture, pulled up in her station wagon and beckoned all of the adults and children to pile in, so they could find the fire.

But when they arrived at a peaceful field on the other end of the island, there was no evidence of a fire.

Watching the retreating fire truck, the family members shrugged and jokingly wondered for what purpose, if any, they had all been brought together in such a pastoral surrounding.

They laughed and returned home.

The phone rang.

It was Bruno.

"Daddy just died," he reported sadly. "A heart attack."

The family was heartsick.

Not until later did Arthur and his brothers determine that the exact time of their father's death was the very moment that the family had been summoned by the false fire alarm to a tranquil setting.

As if God had orchestrated it.

It was years before Arthur consciously tied together the two events relating to his father—the parallel of the story that embarrassed Arthur and caused him to hurt his father's feelings, and the events that day on the island.

He recalled the point of his father's story—that God validates His presence in our lives through small extraordinary events, such as the coincidence of a man's picture being toppled by a gust of wind at the exact moment that man dies. Arthur then connected that memory to the godwink of his father's family being summoned to a peaceful field at the exact moment that his father had died.

"We need to pay attention to these spirit connections in life," said Arthur. "They describe the existence of God—that God *is*, and His mystery is awesome."

:: :: ::

His Personal Way

Mavis, Tim, Daniel, Romaine, and Arthur each received a reassuring and very personal communication from above. Mavis was not expecting a godwink, but it connected her with a long lost child and changed her life. Tim Conway, testing God's existence, received an answer in the form of a glow-in-the-dark cross on a green ribbon that has resonated with him ever since.

Daniel, desperately seeking assurances that his daughter was in heaven, found winks from God that gave him a personal reply. Romaine, secretly wishing her long-deceased mother could share her wedding joy, received a powerful godwink of acknowledgment in learning the likeness between her mother and David's. And for Arthur, it was many years before he linked together two powerful experiences, helping to form a broader perspective and greater appreciation of God's wondrous ways.

> In all your ways
> acknowledge Him,
> And He shall
> direct your paths.
> —PROVERBS 3:6 NKJV

Perhaps you can identify with these stories through parallel experiences of your own—experiences you may have shrugged off or forgotten. Dig into your memory right now. Start taking what I call an archaeological expedition into your past. See if you, too, have received a godwink, delivered at just the right time to assure you that you were not alone—that Someone was up there watching over you in a very personal way.

CHAPTER TWO

WINKS OF HOPE & REASSURANCE

I'm a big fan of simple things, aren't you?

How did I guess? You're holding *this* book, not a thick erudite one.

If you were a kid growing up in America during the '70s or '80s, perhaps you saw some simple programs under my charge at ABC TV. Scheduled in between Saturday morning cartoons, they were three-minute programs called *SchoolHouse Rock* that brought you simple messages through music and animation. They entertainingly taught the parts of speech, such as in "Conjunction Junction"; taught the math tables, including "My Hero Zero"; and included a favorite history program, "Preamble."

At the time it never occurred to me that we were doing

something with lasting value because of its simplicity. No—from my perspective, I was just a young TV exec trying to identify with kids and their ability to process information.

As a side note, my own children laughed at me, saying I was trying to identify with young people *too* much. The month I took over Children's Television at ABC, my dentist advised that the only way to get rid of the David Letterman-space between my front teeth was to wear braces. So there I was, ABC's first vice president in charge of kids programming, wearing braces.

In any case, today I get a great lift when someone tells me that those simple little ABC *SchoolHouse Rock* programs helped them through school. And to prove it, they dig into their memory banks and burst into "I'm just a Bill on Capitol Hill . . ." the story of how a bill goes through Congress, or "Conjunction junction, what's your function?"

I think simple is good.

Don't you cherish the simple moments in life? When you look at the beauty of a butterfly or the intricate construction of a bird's nest with your child? Or when you walk hand-in-hand on a sunset beach with someone you love?

Simple gifts are God's best gifts.

Perhaps I love simple because I grew up in a simple home in northern New York in a small town with a simple name—Adams Center.

People there believed that God communicates with each of us in simple ways. I can still hear the voice of Mama Alice, my rosy-cheeked, large-bosomed grandmother, in her lingering British accent: "Remember dear, God always speaks to you in a small, still voice."

When I began to write the stories about coincidences in all aspects of our lives—history, medicine, sports, relationships—and wondered what they meant, the term "godwink" came into mind and I thought of Mama Alice again—her loving, reassuring wink to me across the dining room table. That's when I heard the small, still voice telling me that a wink from God was the same thing—a sweet, personal communication directly to you; a simple statement of hope and reassurance from God to you.

Perhaps by learning the story of how these *when God winks* books evolved, you will have a clearer picture of how God has built hope and reassurance for me, and how He also works in your life in small, simple ways, often accompanied by His signature—godwinks.

THE LITTLE BOOK THAT COULD

Though it may seem to be, this story is not really about me.

It's about the series of *when God winks* books and the

unbelievable godwinks that lifted them from obscurity to land on Oprah Winfrey's bedroom nightstand.

But I must fully confess, right here and now, that because I have been led to every story in them, each book has been coauthored.

By God and me.

He is the Author.

I just wrote down the stories He gave me.

It all began at the little church on Quaker Hill in upstate New York where I was invited to speak. What a coincidence that I ended up at this church, well off the beaten path. It turned out to be across the road from the country home of my hero, Dr. Norman Vincent Peale, the prominent author of *The Power of Positive Thinking*.

Several months in advance of my talk, I chose a topic that had always fascinated me: "Coincidence: Is It Evidence of a Grand Plan?" Then just days before my talk, Dr. Peale died—on Christmas Eve—and was buried behind that little church, causing me to alter my opening remarks.

"The president of the United States said something this week that resonated with each of us. He said, 'What a coincidence that Dr. Peale, who gave his life to the celebration of Christ, should be called to God's side on the very eve that the world celebrates the *birth* of Christ.' Coincidence? I-e-e-e wonder."

Well, that started it.

Sharing incredible coincidence stories that I encountered over the years connected me with my audience like never before. I was looking into the faces of adults who appeared like children listening to a bedtime story. My audience was engaging me with smiles, nods, and wide-eyed wonder.

I knew then and there that I had come upon a topic that touched people. Somehow I struck a nerve with the question: "Is it possible that coincidence has something to do with God and His grand plan for you?"

I determined from that experience to write a book.

I soon began to learn the cold, hard lessons of becoming an author. If you've ever thought about writing a book, this might be helpful information.

It's a long process.

Finding and developing the discipline to write daily—five to seven every morning before my day job—took me four years to figure out.

Ferreting out the book's "voice" and style took another two years.

Finding a literary agent who believed in it—and me—was in the seventh year.

Getting a publisher to gamble on an unknown author—even though I once ran *Good Morning America,* which clearly impressed *me* much more than it did them—was a "lesson in rejection" into my eighth year.

I had thirty turndowns before a small Northwest publisher, Beyond Words Publishing, took a chance on me and released my first *when God winks* book.

Then there was another awakening. I naively learned that after years of writing, a finished manuscript was only the beginning.

"My publisher's job is to get the book into the store," counseled one veteran author/speaker. "My job is to get it out!"

In that clear, cold assessment, I realized that no matter how excited you think your publisher is about your baby—and its multiyear gestation period—it's just one more book on the company's plate. At Barnes&Noble, where seemingly a million books reside, you're just one more slice of baloney on the shelf.

How does one little book scramble to the top and get attention over all the rest?

Publicity, of course!

And one soon concludes that there's an unspoken expectation that you, the author, will be generating most of that publicity. The publisher may give you some help, a three-month window with a PR person, but then you're generally expected to be on your own. You need to hire your own PR representative and/or make relentless calls to the media.

It is now understandable to me why famous people who are not good writers are more readily published than good writers who are not famous. Having access to TV and radio talk shows and the fortitude to keep plugging away is simply what is expected of you—in addition, of course, to having the manuscript that you've sweated and slaved over.

All right, enough whining about that! Let's get to the big question: How does one get booked on *The Oprah Winfrey Show*?

During the first two years that *when God winks* was on the bookshelves, published by Beyond Words in Portland, I hired four different PR people to make pitches to *Oprah Show* producers. What a thrill it was the day one of the *Oprah* producers called back and said the most enchanting words any author can hear:

"I love your book. Oprah will love your book!"

My heart soared.

One week later was the tragedy of 9/11. All shows for the entire season—*Oprah* and every other talk show—were revamped to deal with a nation in mourning. And no one in the mainstream media could envision the merit of a segment about the inspirational stories in my little book.

I did receive support from *The 700 Club* on the ABC Family Channel and a considerable number of radio programs, but national television turned a deaf ear. People who worked with me when I ran *Good Morning America* were now employed by virtually every major talk show, yet the answer to my PR people was pretty much the same: "Tell SQuire we love him. We hate the title of his book."

Yes, that three-letter word, G-O-D, was the impediment for many bookers. Ironically, the title was the reason so many people said they were drawn to the book in the first place.

Then a major godwink occurred. I was scheduled to appear on the *Hour of Power* at the Crystal Cathedral in Garden Grove, California, on Mother's Day, 2003. I told my publisher that this powerful TV ministry was viewed in more than 150 million homes every Sunday morning.

"You better get a lot more books in the pipeline," I counseled the publisher, Richard Cohn, ever certain that my publisher's maintenance of supply was falling short of my whipping up demand.

"I think we can afford to put five thousand books in the system," said Richard, consulting his checkbook.

"What? That's not enough," I complained.

That's when I realized the downside to a small publisher. While I was elated with Beyond Words's creativity, design, and editorial sense under Editor-in-Chief Cindy Black, and I loved the friendly accessibility to Richard, the ability of most publishing companies to quickly put large numbers of books into the pipeline is dictated by the vagaries of their cash flow. Subsequent to 9/11, through no fault of their own, many of Beyond Words's vendors were considerably late in their payments. My publisher was struggling to find sufficient capital with which to operate.

Looking skyward, I prayerfully complained: "What am I going to do, Lord? I finally get international TV exposure, and there aren't going to be enough books in the stores."

My hopes were crashing.

But my wonderful wife, Louise, had an idea. "We can't let this opportunity pass," she said. "Let's put $20,000 worth of books on our credit card."

Gulp—that was my gulp.

The second gulp came from my publisher.

But when the *Hour of Power* went on the air and *when God winks* shot to number twenty-one on Amazon.com, there were indeed enough books in the stores.

What we didn't know was that our faith in the book was opening the way for another extraordinary godwink to unfold a few weeks later.

Judith Curr, the president of a new Simon & Schuster

imprint, Atria Books, was making the annual pilgrimage—
like most publishers—to Ann Arbor, Michigan, headquarters
of Borders and Waldenbooks. At the conclusion of Judith's
presentation of the new fall catalog, a young woman named
Marcella Clashman came up to her and said perfect words to
a publisher's ears:

> "The book you really ought to get is *when God winks*—
> we can't keep it on the shelf."

Marcella had been monitoring increased book sales every
time there was media attention, particularly after the *Hour of
Power* broadcast.

"What's it about?" asked Judith.

"The power of coincidence in our lives," replied Marcella.

Judith was very attentive. Marcella had no way of knowing
that years before in Australia, Judith Curr became a star in
publishing circles by launching an unknown book called *The
Celestine Prophecy*—all about coincidence.

Marcella's perfect words, striking the perfect ears, was an
incredible godwink.

That was on a Friday. The following Monday an offer was
placed on the table to license from Beyond Words the right to
publish an Atria Books / Simon & Schuster edition of *when*

God winks. There was never again a question of having enough books in the stores.

Oprah continued to be in our prayers. An appearance on *The Oprah Winfrey Show* was what the book needed to get it into the national consciousness. When you think of it, Oprah's name probably shows up in more daily prayers than anyone else in the country.

Mostly authors' prayers.

By 2004, I felt I had made some real progress. I was told that a specific producer had been assigned to *when God winks.* Ahh . . . finally there was someone my PR people could bug.

But on the morning of May 9, 2004, I saw myself like a little kid trudging to the end of the line with my baseball hat in my hand. *Oprah* was winding down for the season. In just three weeks, it would go into summer hiatus. I knew in my heart that I would have to wait until the show started up again in September. Again, my hopes plummeted.

"I don't think we're going to make it this year," I grumbled to my wife, Louise, as we finished our morning prayer time.

Brightly, she looked at me and said with authority: "If God wants you on that show, He'll find a way!"

Because I tend to believe everything my wonderful wife says, I nodded, accepted, and perhaps for the first time, let go—and let God.

Three days later, we were driving through Virginia Beach, Virginia, where Louise travels one week a month to tape her talk show, *Living the Life* (ABC Family Channel).

My cell phone rang. It was a woman's voice—a friend, breathless with excitement.

"Oprah just held up your book!" she said quickly.

My eyes squinted. Slowly, I shook my head, and looked at the phone as I said good-bye.

"She's obviously mistaken," I said to Louise, "probably has it confused with someone else's book."

Then three more calls, including Richard Cohn, my first publisher. The same message.

We were astounded.

Here's what happened: Oprah was giving her TV audience a tour of her Chicago home. Entering a bedroom, she mentioned that rather than having a TV in that room, she liked to keep favorite books by the bed. She reached down and picked up the top one.

"I have a book called *when God winks* . . . I love that . . . cute little stories about how there are no coincidences in our life."

Oprah set the book down and went on with her tour. But on Amazon.com and Barnes&Noble there was a flurry of activity. The book shot into the top ten in a matter of hours.

A few weeks later, Louise and I were at home to see the

rerun of the show, sitting right where I had "let go and let God." As we sat before the TV, eagerly anticipating that Oprah was going to pick up my little book and that it was again going to zoom into the top ten, the bigger question—the one that really fascinated us—was, *How did God get my book into Oprah's bedroom just three days after our prayer?*

Unquestionably, the taping of Oprah's visit to her home occurred many days or weeks before Louise and I uttered our prayer. One can only conclude that from God's perspective, it's just part of His much larger yet simple plan. God's simple plan to provide hope and reassurance.

Think about it. Where would my little *when God winks* books be today without all those god-winks? The ironic connection between my original pulpit talk at a little country church and Dr.

> I have good plans for you, not plans to hurt you. I will give you hope and a good future.
> —JEREMIAH 29:11 NCV

Peale's death on Christmas Eve, the "perfect words" spoken by a young book buyer to the "perfect ears," and the incredible godwink of the book ending up in Oprah's bedroom just three days after we had "let go and let God." They are all downright baffling.

So many times in life, we look plaintively skyward, uttering frustration or a complaint. We think we aren't being heard. But we are. Our complaint is a prayer that God hears and truly understands. He just may have a plan to answer it differently than we expected.

My plan was to be a guest on Oprah's show. God's plan was different—an unsolicited endorsement for my book—Oprah saying, "I love it."

In the final analysis, I wasn't the only benefactor of God's blessings. Beyond Words, my publisher who had faith in the godwinks concept and developed the original *when God winks* book, received blessings as well. Richard Cohn and Cindy Black acquired the rights to a book called *The Hidden Messages in Water* by a Japanese researcher named Masaru Emoto and subsequently watched the book hit the *New York Times* bestseller list. And to top it off, Judith Curr—my publisher at Simon & Schuster's Atria Books—who got to know Richard and Cindy through our experience, offered Beyond Words a deal to become a new imprint of S&S.

> All journeys have secret destinations of which the traveler is unaware.[1]
> —MARTIN BUBER

God's overall plan for you and me is so much bigger than our small, simple minds can possibly comprehend. When we demonstrate our faith in Him, He provides us with hope and reassurance, revealing a portion of His plan for us.

WALK OF FAME WINK

Fred Travalena is an incredible impressionist. He conducts a conversation between nine presidents—with voices from JFK to George W.—that makes your head spin. He also sings like Tony Bennett and Frank Sinatra; you'd swear they were right there onstage.

The time Fred wished he could truly *be* somebody else was when he found out that a tennis-ball-sized lymphoma had formed in his abdomen—cancer. Every conceivable thought rushed into his mind:

Why me?
What will this do to my career?
How long is it going to take us to lick it, God?

He knew he had to focus on the finish line. That's why, as he commenced treatment on June 5, 2002, it resonated with him when the nurse holding his chart said: "You're going to love the day I write down N.E.D."

"What's that?"

"No Evidence of Disease."

That's how Fred made it through weeks of chemo that sapped his strength and stole his hair. He and his wife, Lois, "kept God on the line," entering into prayer more times a day than ever before, riveting their positive attention on total healing.

Seven months along his road to recovery, a writer called and said he wanted to do a magazine story. Fred wrestled with that, wondering if publicity of his cancer would harm his ability to secure work in the future—you never know why a talent booker might turn you down. But then, he wanted to help others who might find themselves in his shoes. So he decided he'd give the interview.

Months went by; nothing happened with the story. Apparently, no magazine had picked it up, and it drifted from memory.

Fred continued to make what his doctors called *remarkable progress.* His daily regimen of prayer and nutrition to augment medical science was working. On June 5, 2003—one year to the day that he had started his fight—he had a doctor's appointment. The nurse smiled as she pointed to the three letters on Fred's chart: N.E.D. No Evidence of Disease.

"You can't imagine the elation I felt," said Fred. "The first call I made was to the Man Upstairs. I said, 'Thank you, God.'"

On the way home, he received a return call—a godwink—at a magazine stand. There, in *The National Enquirer* magazine, was Fred's story, published exactly one year to the day that he'd begun his victorious battle against cancer.

"That was a real booster from the Lord," said Fred, still concealing those moments when he'd secretly wondered if he was going to survive. "That godwink gave me hope."

There are times in life when we get a double whammy we just can't explain. Three months later, Fred was diagnosed with another form of cancer. Prostate cancer. He immediately underwent surgery while Lois reactivated the prayer chains.

Twice Fred Travalena faced the battle of cancer.

Twice he was the victor.

Being out of circulation for any length of time in the entertainment business, where dates are booked many months in advance, can cripple career momentum.

At a family gathering in spring 2004, Fred's two sons were kicking around ideas to help their dad revive his entertainment schedule. Freddy, Jr. had a wild idea.

"Hey Dad. Why don't you get a star on Hollywood Boulevard?"

"Oh sure," said Fred. "Just like that!"

His son shrugged and smiled. "Why not?" he said softly.

It was a big idea, thought Fred. *Only a couple of thousand people had ever been given that honor. Such a thing would let people know he was back, in great shape.*

"Just thought I'd throw it out there," continued Freddy, Jr.

"Tell you what," said Fred, "I'll make one call—to Johnny Grant, the honorary mayor of Hollywood—to find out what it takes."

> Count it all joy when you fall into various trials, knowing that the testing of your faith produces patience.
>
> —JAMES 1:2–3 NKJV

He was surprised. Johnny Grant came right on the line. Fred asked his question: How does someone get nominated for a star on the Walk of Fame?

"Your timing is impeccable," bubbled Johnny over the phone. "I'm just going in to our annual nomination meeting. If you'd called fifteen minutes later, you'd be too late—you'd have to wait 'til next year."

He laughed.

Fred hung up the phone. Converting his face into Goober from *The Andy Griffith Show*, he said: "Hey—maybe we got a shot."

In June 2004, two years after Fred had faced and conquered cancer with God's help and excellent doctors—twice—he once again stopped at a newsstand. This time he picked up a newspaper to find this joyous news: Fred Travalena was to be one of the celebrities honored with a star on the Hollywood Boulevard Walk of Fame the following February 3rd, star number 2277.

Fred and Lois reflect that their faith has grown stronger. And they know that God will use Fred's experience in overcoming cancer to help others come to the Lord.

Moreover, with clarity of hindsight, they see that the godwink of *The National Enquirer* story happening one year to the day of his commencement of treatment, and the godwink of making the phone call about the star on Hollywood Boulevard exactly one year after that, within fifteen minutes of the key person going into a nomination meeting, were extraordinary messages of hope and reassurance from the Almighty . . . that Fred Travalena will be around for a long time.

CATCHING HOPE

Hope is a powerful force in life. It's like going into the kitchen, turning on the faucet, and being surprised by the water pressure. You almost jump back, giddy that there's so much energy pouring out.

Your hope is stored up inside and wants to burst out of you the same way. You need to turn on the faucet of your faith and then feel the surge of hope that springs forth.

If you are fully hopeful, you'll cause other people around you to almost jump, happily splashed with your enthusiasm.

Reinforced by the wonderful godwinks that happen to you, hope is contagious. Go ahead. Spread it around!

MYSTERY PHOTO

"I was searching. Even though my life was in a good place—fairly happy—I was searching for direction," said Lisa Gilpin.

She and her husband Sandy had been earnestly trying to get pregnant, but their continued disappointment raised unspoken doubts. Would they be able to have a baby? Was there something wrong with one of them?

Then there was the nagging career question. What direction? Should she go back to school or stay the course in the workplace?

Thank God for the church tour to the Holy Land. It would be a welcome distraction. Organized by fellow members of New York's Marble Collegiate Church, accompanied by their pastor, Dr. Arthur Caliandro, Lisa and Sandy were looking forward to exploring ancient places of the Bible and walking where Jesus had walked.

As they arrived in Israel, Lisa's personal uncertainties seemed thousands of miles away—six thousand, to be exact.

Early in the trip was a journey to Jerusalem. From there the group boarded a bus for an excursion to the ancient biblical town of Jericho. But before they could depart, the bus broke down.

"We have to wait. Another bus is coming to replace this one," shrugged the driver.

> Deep within you ... nothing is hopeless. You are a child of God, and hope has been planted in you by God.[2]
>
> —NORMAN VINCENT PEALE

After a frustrating and seemingly interminable delay, the second bus arrived and they got under way. As they approached the first scheduled rest stop, the driver further irritated his captives by electing to pass it by.

"It was too crowded," he said to his groaning passengers, whose impatience was escalating as rapidly as their need to visit a restroom.

"There's another stop a few miles ahead," he added.

When the bus finally did roll into a rest stop, Lisa bolted down the steps, heading directly for the ladies' room as quickly as possible.

The men's and the women's rooms were separated by a partition and identified in both English and Arabic. As one additional distinguishing characteristic, on the door for women was a picture of a lady.

Thankfully, Lisa was one of the first to rush into the restroom. But as she exited, she found that a line had formed and the women had broken into an excited titter.

Lisa was the subject of all their attention.

Excitedly they pointed to the woman's picture on the ladies' room door. It was a picture of *her!*

Her?

Yes.

Looking more closely than her urgings of nature had previously permitted, Lisa looked at her face in a photo taken twenty years earlier, when she was a nineteen-year-old college student. Her memory rushed to that moment in her life—another time of searching because of an uncertain relationship with a boyfriend—and she recalled the day that she had been asked to pose for a Red Cross volunteer poster.

"How did your picture get here?" animatedly asked the other women.

"I . . . don't know. It must be some kind of joke," she replied, almost dazed. Her mind was racing, wondering if, as a gag, someone could have preceded them to the rest stop.

Her pastor, Arthur Caliandro, joined the gathering to see what all the fuss was about.

"Is this a joke, Arthur?" asked Lisa.

He, too, was momentarily stunned . . . shook his head, and replied with a wide-eyed smile: "No. It's no joke, Lisa."

How did Lisa's picture end up at an unscheduled country-side rest stop, in a land she'd never visited, six thousand miles from home?

No one knows.

In subsequent years, Arthur asked Lisa several times: "How do you interpret that experience?"

"I don't know. I don't know," was always her reply.

Before leaving the rest stop that day in the countryside of Israel, Lisa asked the manager if she could have the picture. He gave it to her. And every time she looked at it, she thought long and hard about the power of the godwink that she experienced. Only through the distance of time and greater insight has the event become clearer. She now realizes that at the time the god-wink occurred, she was unknowingly crossing the bridge from a time of uncertainty into a pleasant place of certainty. Her searching was coming to an end.

Shortly after Lisa and Sandy returned to America, she was overcome with the kind of joy that could originate only from the Almighty—with an assurance that her prayers had indeed been heard. She was able to tell her family and friends that she was pregnant. She later gave birth to a beautiful baby boy.

During the same period, Lisa began to have clarity about the direction of her career. She reenrolled in school and earned a master's degree in social work.

> Nothing can be done without hope or confidence.[3]
>
> —HELEN KELLER

God's wink had been a reaffirmation of His presence in her life.

Dr. Caliandro agreed: "Your experience describes the existence of God; a demonstration that there is something beyond us. It's mystery, it's awesome, and we need to pay attention to it."

GOD'S FLIGHT PLAN

John Francis knew about crossroads.

"I'll keep you in my prayers," he said to Ron Mechlin, a member of his congregation whom he had just asked how things were going. He knew Ron was in a highly dangerous profession as a Boeing test pilot.

"We're at a crossroads," said Ron. "This week we're testing a new rear rotor for helicopters."

Something from the writings of Herbert O'Driscoll skittered

across John's mind: *Crossroads call for choices, and the choices we make will change the pattern of our lives. God and the devil are both waiting at the crossroads, each attempting to direct one's paths, to heaven or to hell.*

Grasping Ron's hand, John repeated himself.

"I'll keep you in my prayers."

Just three years into his tenure as the pastor of a church outside of Philadelphia, John was at a crossroads of his own on some sticky issues; he had to make a stand on controversial policies of the church. That worried him. Would the outcome of his choices keep him in good favor with his congregation? Would he also be serving God in the manner expected of him?

A day or two later, John was a bit cranky that he'd been delayed by four hours in a drive to a summer cottage on the eastern shore of Virginia. He wondered if he were annoyed with his tardiness or just troubled by the tough choices looming before him. His mind went to a book he'd read that paralleled everyday choices with the choices Dorothy had to make in *The Wizard of Oz*—at each crossroads, she was challenged by the forces of good and evil.

Was he making the right choices as he traveled his own "yellow brick road"?

"God, please give me a sign," he said out loud.

Just then, John was approaching one of several milestones along his frequent drive to the house at the shore—New Castle Airport. He had a sudden, inexplicable urge to turn into the airport. As he did so, he heard sirens, people were running, and he saw smoke rising from a runway.

Internally, he felt a "powerful push" to get out of the car and run to the wreckage.

He knew that New Castle Airport was a National Guard facility, and it came back to him that he'd heard that the airfield was also used as a test facility.

He encountered a military guard post.

"I've got to get over there," he said to the MP at the gate. "I'm the pastor of a church. I think one of my parishioners needs me."

The guard looked at him up and down. John was wearing blue jeans and a T-shirt—hardly the attire of a pastor.

The guard paused and with a doubtful expression motioned John to pass through.

The fire engine and ambulance were already at the site of the wreckage. It was as he suspected . . . a helicopter. Someone was being pulled free. It was Ron Mechlin, his friend the test pilot. John spoke to an emergency worker, learning that, fortunately, Ron suffered only a broken arm and minor injuries.

Following the ambulance to the hospital, John was able to be at Ron's side, to contact his wife, and to comfort the two of them.

Later that day as John continued his journey along his own "yellow brick road" to the Virginia shore, he realized that at his crossroads, he'd asked for and received a sign from God —an extraordinary wink from above that caused him to be delayed by four hours, placing him at the New Castle Airport just when God wanted him there. And the powerful push to go to the crash site, where he would find Ron Mechlin in a helicopter

> Man is a creature of hope and invention, both of which belie the idea that things cannot be changed.[4]
>
> —TOM CLANCY

crash, was God's way of confirming His presence at John's crossroads.

THE INCREDIBLE, UNBELIEVABLE CALL

Uncertainty was pressing on Ken Gaub.

Self-pity enshrouded him.

What do you want with me, Lord? he silently demanded as

the family's two Silver Eagle motor coaches traveled along I-75 somewhere near Dayton, Ohio.

Ken's two sons were driving, keeping in touch with a CB radio. The rest of the family members were snoozing, reading, or lost in their own reverie.

"Let's make a stop at that exit," radioed one son to the other.

The Gaub family was a traveling ministry, covering fifty thousand miles a year, taking their family entertainment act into churches, schools, and on the back roads of America.

Ken was feeling tired. Unsatisfied.

Where am I, Lord?

He wondered about his purpose.

Couldn't we serve you better by staying put—making a lot more money to support other ministries? Lost in thought, Ken was almost unaware that the family had decided to take a break and had pulled up to a small-town diner.

"You go ahead," he said to the others. "I'm just gonna stretch and take a walk."

He crossed through a gas station, walking past an empty phone booth. Suddenly it began to ring.

He stopped. Looked around. It kept ringing.

He started to step away.

He paused again.

What if it's for the gas station attendant? he thought, looking around for someone who might be the target of some unknown caller. *Maybe it's an emergency.*

That consideration caused him to step into the booth.

"Hello?"

"I have a person to person call for Mr. Ken Gaub," said the operator.

"What?" said Ken, instinctively furrowing his brow, and looking around for the *Candid Camera* TV crew that surely must be lurking somewhere . . . with a fake telephone operator . . . calling an empty phone booth . . . trying to trap him looking silly . . . by asking for *him.*

"Calling Ken Gaub," repeated the operator.

"You're crazy," he retorted, once again doing a 360-degree scan for the hidden cameras.

Less patiently, the operator asked, "Is this Ken Gaub?"

"Yeeess . . ."

"I have a person-to-person call for you," she reiterated, with the tone of a teacher scolding a child.

"I believe that's him," said another voice on the phone—a woman's voice.

Now Ken was really curious. If this were a setup, it was a really good job.

"Go ahead," said the operator dismissively.

"Mr. Gaub, I saw you on a TV show, *The 700 Club,*" said

the woman, with a quick nervousness. "I'm Millie . . . I live in Harrisburg . . . and . . . I remembered your name and wrote it into a letter I was writing . . . a . . . suicide note . . ."

The woman began to cry.

Ken was puzzled.

"You don't know me . . . but I'm desperate . . . I remembered you . . . and a phone number came into my mind to call you. Thank you so much for taking my call."

This was no joke, concluded Ken.

"*How* did you get this number?" he asked, shaking his head.

"I . . . I don't know. It just came into my mind, while I was writing. Is this in your office? In California?"

"Ma'am, my office is in Yakima, Washington, but that's not where I am."

"Where are you?" she sniffled.

"Millie, you called *me*. I'm in a phone booth at a gas station in Dayton!"

"Oh. What are you doing there?"

"Answering the phone," he said with a chuckle, beginning to enjoy the experience.

"Can I talk with you?"

"Yes. Of course."

For the next ten minutes they talked. Ken assured her that the Lord was watching over her, that her worries were only temporary, that turning to God was the only answer. In Him, she would find peace. For after all . . . He had already led her to him.

Saying good-bye, Ken took a seat on a stone wall by the gas station. For several moments he contemplated the power of the godwink that he and Millie had just experienced.

Was this a message of hope for her, or a message of hope for me? he silently asked the Almighty.

Across the asphalt driveway, he saw his wife and the others emerging from the diner.

"Hey, Barb!" he shouted, giddy with delight. "Hey! God knows where I am!"

So many times over the years, Ken Gaub has revisited that personal, life-changing godwink.

"I don't believe it, and it happened to me!" he says. "What are the astronomical odds that I would get that call from Millie?"

Time after time he has reflected on how that experience not only stopped Millie from taking an irreversible step but also how, from that day on, all of the uncertainty about his purpose in life was suddenly lifted from his shoulders.

Ken also recalls that a few months later, after the family performed in Harrisburg, a smiling woman came up to him and said: "Hi. I'm Millie!"

Funny, she looked pretty much as he imagined she would.

There were a few subsequent telephone and letter communications, and then Ken lost touch. She was no longer listed in the Harrisburg directories. She must have moved away.

But, who knows?

Maybe she'll call again sometime.

HANDING OUT HOPE

Probably like you, I have saved certain notes from people through the years that gave me a lift. I have one from a boss at a big radio station in Boston where I had my first producing job. In a handwritten note he said: "Nice going on Sunday's show."

That's all—five words on a small piece of paper. But that note gave me the reassurance that I was doing okay, that I was performing up to par, that he noticed and appreciated my work. That gave me hope, and hope was the fuel that propelled me onward, to work even harder.

You've no doubt received a complimentary comment from someone that did the same for you—gave you a boost, lifted your spirits, and made you feel good.

How about doing the same for someone today? Think what a lasting value your comment will have, particularly if years from now your hope note still exists in someone's box of memorabilia.

CHAPTER THREE

GOD WINKS ON TRANSITIONS

At times of transition in your life, you seem out of sorts—lost.

Something happens to you unexpectedly, turning everything upside down. You realize that things are never going to be the same again. A feeling creeps over you—as uncertainty invades your mind, you have the terrible feeling of a loss of control.

When you lose someone or something you love, the stages of mourning begin to unfold: Shock. Anger. Sadness.

You wonder how you can possibly get along.

Often at these times, God winks at you. Through a coincidental experience or answered prayer, He sends you a hopeful message—just as real as placing His arm around you—providing you with a concrete connection to Him.

THE SMILE OF THE SAD-FACED CLOWN

Stasia Kelly was in shock.

She sat on the plane bound from Denver to Sarasota, gazing at the picture of her father on the front page of the morning newspaper. "Emmett Kelly, World's Most Famous Clown, Dead at 80."

She looked at her father's famous countenance—the sad-faced hobo, Weary Willie. That was his trademark. All the other clowns in the circus wore wide grins. But Willie's sad face was so compelling, so endearing, it made him stand out.

Stasia's mind raced to the night before. The phone conversation with her dad was out of character. He was so talkative—so unusually expressive as he reminisced about his life.

For twenty years he had performed with Ringling Bros. and Barnum & Bailey Circus. Despite the adoration of the crowds, it was a solitary life. For when the tent went down and he boarded the train for the next town, he was all alone. His only family was the circus.

Then in his fifties, he caught sight of Evi, Stasia's mom. She was a tiny-waisted acrobat from Germany. He was smitten right away.

"As Weary Willie, I would amble over to the ring where she was performing and pretend to fall asleep," recalled her dad over the phone. "But what I was really doing was lifting one eye so I could catch a glimpse of your beautiful mother." He giggled.

Stasia's dad told her it took him a while to work up the courage to ask Evi to marry him. "But it was the happiest day of my life," said her dad, "except for the day you were born."

Stasia noted the change in his voice as he began to talk about that day.

She had long known the family legend. Her sad-faced father—Weary Willie—so carefully guarded his trademark face that he never allowed himself to be caught smiling in a photograph.

Except for that one time.

Her father recalled the significance of that day. During a publicity interview with a UPI photographer, the phone rang. It was Evi's doctor.

"Congratulations! You're the father of a baby daughter," said the doctor. Involuntarily Weary Willie's face burst into a huge smile—from ear to ear.

Click.

That picture of the sad-faced clown smiling, the photographer's best shot ever—a godwink itself—went around the world to newspapers everywhere.

Stasia's father seemed overjoyed every time he told the story.

Turning from the airplane window, Stasia looked down at the picture of her father on the front page of another newspaper she'd grabbed to bring with her at the last minute—an old yellowed newspaper with a photo of Weary Willy. The one and only one that caught him smiling.

Notwithstanding all the times she'd seen it before, she now had a sudden understanding: it struck her what he was smiling about.

Her!

Her arrival into his life!

Quietly, Stasia began to cry.

A man seated next to her, leaned over. He asked if she was all right.

"Yes," she whispered. "My father died this morning," pointing to the picture in her lap.

The man's face turned ashen.

"You're not going to believe this!" he stammered. "I was with your father the day you were born. I took that picture!"

Stasia looked at him, puzzled.

"I'm Frank Beatty. The UPI photographer. That was the only picture ever taken of your dad smiling."

Instantly, a peace flowed over her. It was as though this incredible wink from God was delivered at this very moment to bring comfort, that her daddy was at God's side—looking down on her.

Stasia Kelly and Frank Beatty became close friends. Five years later, he was the photographer who took her wedding pictures when she became Mrs. Steve Woodburn.

At the wedding, they talked about one other godwink. Emmett Kelly died of a heart attack on the most important day of the year for any clown—March 28—the day the Ringling Bros. and Barnum & Bailey Circus always opened its annual show at Madison Square Garden in New York.

:: :: ::

GRADUATION FROM LIFE

When you lose someone you love, godwinks seem to occur more frequently. Perhaps you are more sensitive, more attuned to God's messages at those moments. But godwinks are always there for those who are open to receiving them. They are there to help you through transitions, to bolster you up, to give you strength, to let you know you're not alone.

I have an idea about these kinds of transitions. We all are going to graduate one way or the other, and as with all graduations, the saddest people are not the graduates but those who are left behind.

> Now we know that if the earthly tent we live in is destroyed, we have a building from God, an eternal house in heaven, not built by human hands.
>
> —2 CORINTHIANS 5:1 NIV

According to the Scriptures, "Those who believe in the Son have eternal life,"[1] and the graduate who has asked the Lord to prepare the way is already thinking about new horizons—and if given the choice, would choose not to return, not even to come back to be with us.

A YELLOW SEA OF TAXIS

Diane Lane's black limo snaked through New York City traffic, taking her to the studios where Charlie Rose tapes his nightly talk show.

Through the backseat window her eyes followed darting yellow taxicabs—more than she could count—as her thoughts drifted to childhood, growing up in this city of fifteen thousand taxicabs.

In her memory, she saw herself as an excited preteen, standing at the school curb, straining through the maze of yellow cabs, always looking for that special one—number 6F99. That was her dad's. At 2:45 PM, he'd flip on his "Off Duty" light and arrive at her school like a yellow chariot. Diane would be a princess among her peers, picked up in her own special car—a limousine of sorts.

Long after he sold his cab when she was sixteen, Diane would always scan the New York horizon of yellow cars, looking for, but never again finding, number 6F99.

How life had changed since those schoolgirl days!

And oh, how her dad would have loved driving her today! He'd get a kick out of people recognizing her on the streets, now that she'd grown into an accomplished Hollywood actress.

She imagined him coming into the studio with her, sitting off to the side, quietly bursting with pride for his little girl as she talked with Charlie Rose about her new movie, *Unfaithful.*

Exhaling a soft sigh, she dabbed moisture from the corners of her eyes as her memory replayed her dad's voice that day he called: "How strong are you?" It turned out, stronger than she thought. Strong enough to spend hours and hours with him at the hospital. Strong enough to feel him die in her arms, overtaken by cancer.

Seeing her own reflection in the limo window, she caught herself smiling—thinking of the two of them on the couch before the TV, watching one of his favorite shows, *Charlie Rose*.

Yes, her dad would have really enjoyed being there with her today.

Her car pulled to the curb at the PBS studio.

A surge of breath suddenly swooped into her lungs as Diane's eyes widened. She was transfixed on the cab pulling from the curb just ahead of them.

It was medallion number 6F99! Her dad's old number.

"Thinking of that day makes my toes wiggle," says Diane. "It makes me feel giddy and filled with a kind of faith that has to do with my father still being with me, supporting me, slapping me on the back and saying, 'Hey, kiddo, you can do this! I'm proud of you, I'm with you.'"

A MUTT NAMED MOE

"You can never give back as much love as a dog gives you," said Chuck McCann, the comedic film and TV actor with the friendly, boyish face. He was reminiscing about the black Lab-and-beagle mongrel that once rode next to him in his SUV.

"The first time I saw him, there was almost a pileup on Ventura Boulevard," recalled Chuck, describing the morning he left a breakfast meeting in Studio City, California, just as a spry, undersized black Lab bounced into traffic.

"I pulled my SUV diagonally across the street, blocking traffic to make sure he wasn't hit, and watched him dart down a side street."

Then, leaving a cacophony of beeping horns behind, he drove down the side street, looking for the little dog.

Chuck parked his truck and started jogging down some steps into a park. He slipped and fell.

"Ow."

Sprawled on the steps, he pulled up a pant leg to assess the injury—a skinned knee. He dabbed it with a handkerchief. And he felt a wet, cold tongue run across his cheek.

"Hey there, fella. I'm okay. Are you okay? C'mon with me . . . we'll see if we can get you back home."

The dog jumped into the truck right next to Chuck and later accompanied his new best friend as he plastered posters around the neighborhood: "Found: Small Black Lab."

The next day Chuck received a phone call. A lady said the dog sounded like a mutt that she, too, had once found and returned to its owner. She had a number. Chuck called it, leaving a message saying that he may have found their dog.

Six days passed.

Finally, a woman telephoned. "Yes, that sounds like our dog," she said in an unemotional monotone. "We were moving to a new house. He was playing in the yard and must have run off."

"What's his name?" asked Chuck, with a slight trace of annoyance that the woman had no expression of concern.

"Moe."

Chuck turned from the phone and yelled, "Moe!"

At that instant, the happy, tail-wagging black Lab dashed into the room.

"Yep. That's your dog," said Chuck. "Didn't you get my message from last week?"

"Yeeess . . ." said the woman with some hesitancy, "but we were moving, and I thought he'd be all right where he was."

Chuck stared at the phone.

"Ma'am if you don't want the dog, I'll keep him."

"All right," she said.

That was how Moe came to be Chuck's permanent best friend. They were inseparable. Everywhere Chuck went, Moe went. And Moe always had his favorite spot in the truck—right next to Chuck.

They were best pals for ten years.

Then one day Moe seemed to be out of sorts. He wasn't his normal, friendly, frisky self. Instead of jumping up when Chuck came into the room, he'd lay there. Sad looking.

"What's the matter, Moe boy? We've got to get you to the doctor."

"It's a stomach disorder," explained the vet. "All we can do is prescribe a medication to try to prevent the disease from spreading."

Chuck was worried. And he knew he was only buying time. Two years passed, and toward the end, Chuck sadly watched the slow deterioration of his beloved dog.

"I'm sorry," said the vet. "We've done all we can."

A constriction swelled in Chuck's throat as tears welled in his eyes. The inevitable hit him like a ton of bricks.

Finally, cradled in Chuck's arms, Moe went to sleep. And never woke up.

The next ten months of mourning were unbearable. Every time Chuck climbed into his SUV, he missed Moe scrambling to be at his side. Every time he walked to the door, he missed Moe jumping up to accompany him. Every time he climbed into bed, he missed the weight of Moe leaping in behind him.

Chuck and his wife, Betty, had other dogs. Four of them—

all rescued one way or another. They were all nice dogs. But . . . he really missed Moe.

One Saturday afternoon, Chuck and Betty were with a friend who needed to stop by Johnny Carson Park. He had to see someone.

An adoption dog show was going on, with rescue groups looking for new homes for their animals. As they passed a booth featuring Lhasa apsos, one particular dog came right up to Chuck.

"He's like a small bag of feathers," said Chuck with surprise, lifting the tiny dog with its soft fur and a face that belonged on a stuffed toy.

He felt a warm, indescribable connection with the dog. He brought him up close and spotted something unusual: the dog had one blue eye and one brown.

"This is the cutest dog I've ever seen," said Chuck to a lady with the rescue group. "What's his name?"

"Moe."

The world stopped. Or so it seemed. Chuck was astonished. He momentarily stared at the woman.

"What did you say?"

"His name is Moe," she repeated.

Chuck and Betty couldn't believe their ears.

"I . . . I've got to have this dog," he said.

The lady smiled, shrugging slightly. "Put your name on the list," she said perfunctorily. "About a hundred others also want him."

"But, I've got to have this dog," Chuck insisted. "Honest . . . we'd provide a wonderful home for him."

"Look! Look how we've bonded," he said, stroking the dog's soft little head.

Unaccustomed to such persistence, the woman started asking questions.

"Well . . . where would he sleep?"

"On my bed, of course," replied Chuck, with an air of wouldn't-everybody-know-that. "We have a house built for dogs. They just let us stay there," continued Chuck, trying to score some points with humor. "They have their own door. They come and go as they please into a dog run. Please . . . come visit our home and see for yourself."

Later that day, that's what the lady did.

Satisfied that Chuck and Betty could indeed provide a wonderful home, the woman placed the little Lhasa apso with one blue eye and one brown into Chuck's arms—a little,

> God blesses those who mourn, for they will be comforted.
>
> —MATTHEW 5:4 NLT

six-month-old "bag of feathers" with the unbelievable name of Moe.

"I'll always miss my first Moe," said Chuck, "but this little Moe is filling a big hole in my heart."

THE BIG PICTURE

Why do we grieve the loss of a pet as much as the loss of some people? It is not at all absurd. We create friendships with animals—as Chuck did with Moe—that are as strong or stronger than some human relationships. So it is very natural to experience the same deep sense of loss and sadness. And the godwinks at the time of these transitions are comforting messages that in God's big picture—from His perspective—it all does make sense.

MICHELLE'S POEM

An image kept popping into Michelle's mind. It made her want to write a poem even though she had limited experience writing poetry.

In her image, there were an old man and an old woman, very much in love but no longer able to be together. The man reminded Michelle of her grandfather with whom she had a deep connection and who had recently become ill.

The poem haunted her. Throughout the summer, Michelle dabbled at it.

"I'd put the poem away then bring it out, fiddle with it. But it just wasn't working," she said.

> The sun, like a Father's hand on His child,
> gently guides him on . . .

Returning to her senior year of college, Michelle took on a heavy load of writing classes, including her first poetry class, and her mind revisited her unfinished poem.

An Elvis song in a TV commercial gave her an inspiration. She thought it would be a great title for her poem: "Return to Sender." Then, despite her pressing study schedule, she had an overwhelming notion.

"I was badgered by the feeling that I had to stop everything to go write my poem, right then," she said.

She turned off the TV and wrote and wrote.

The phone rang.

"It was my father. He called to tell me . . . my grandfather had just died."

Michelle Kowalski reflected on that day and the godwink

of her compulsion to write the poem just as her grandfather was passing from this world to the next.

"I feel God was trying to prepare me, and I was so at peace with it."

From time to time, she still tweaks her poem, but "Return to Sender" is nearly done.

One stanza seems to say it all:

The sun, like a Father's hand on His child, gently guides him
   on, slowly dipping below the horizon, casting deep oranges
   and reds and autumn onto the woman's face.
He smiles, lifts two trembling fingers to his lips
   and blows her a kiss.
He reaches slowly for the brim of his hat,
   as an old cowboy would, and walks on.

HIS EYE IS ON THE SPARROW AND ME

For John thomas Oaks, who spells his middle name in lower-case, music of the church has always been "uppercase" in his life. His dad was a preacher, and great old hymns were at the foundation of his musical education.

Now he was taking day courses at the BMI Musical Theater

Workshop, lugging his keyboard and equipment to coffee shop gigs in New York City in the evenings.

The warm lighting and ambience of Starbucks on Broadway at 51st was an inviting attraction for people seeking relief from the sudden November cold snap. The voices of John and his percussionist rose from the chatter of after-work New Yorkers and the hubbub behind the counter.

He sang an R&B hit from 1972: "If you don't know me by now, you'll never, never, never know me."[2]

John noticed another voice had joined theirs. A nearby woman had closed her eyes and was absently singing along. The song ended to a smattering of polite applause.

"I hope you didn't mind my joining in," said the woman apologetically.

"No, no . . ." said John. "Glad to have the company. Would you like to sing something yourself?"

She looked unsure.

"What are you in the mood to sing?" encouraged John.

"Do you know any hymns?" she asked.

John's face lit into a smile. "I cut my teeth on hymns. Name one."

"Oh, I don't know," she hesitated. "You pick one."

"How about . . . 'His Eye Is on the Sparrow'?"

For a moment, she was quiet, her eyes averted, then she nodded, saying softly: "Yeah. Let's do that one."

The woman stood. Allowing for John's two-bar setup, she began.

Her voice, strong and melodic, floated above the hissing and gurgling of the cappuccino maker and the clatter of chatter. The new voice caught customers' attention. It was a beautiful voice. The café began to quiet.

The woman was now one with the music. John's keyboard accompaniment was one with her.

The song became louder. Not because of the woman, but because everyone in the café was listening intently. Work stopped. Customers turned. The cappuccino maker quieted.

> I sing because I'm happy.
> I sing because I'm free.
> For His eye is on the sparrow
> And I know He watches me.[3]

The song ended and the applause crescendoed to a deafening level.

Shyly she thanked her audience and turned to John thomas with a soft smile.

"That was beautiful," he said.

"Well . . . it's funny you picked that particular hymn," she said.

< 76 >

"Really?"

Moisture glistened in her eyes as she reached to shake John's hand—holding it, then squeezing it.

"That was my daughter's favorite song. She was sixteen . . . she died of a brain tumor last week."

John looked at her, momentarily stunned.

"Are you going to be okay?"

"Yes, I've just got to keep trusting the Lord and singing His songs, and everything's gonna be okay."

Within moments, the woman was gone. John was back to his playing. But his mind ruminated the gift he had been given.

> No eye has seen,
> no ear has heard,
> and no mind has
> imagined what God
> has prepared for
> those who love him.
>
> —1 CORINTHIANS 2:9 NLT

God's eye is surely on the sparrow, but that evening at Starbucks, God's arm was around a woman hurting with grief. He gave her a comforting wink of hope and reassurance and allowed John thomas to be her Godwink Link by suggesting her daughter's favorite song.

For years, John has thought about the dozens of other hymns he could have selected that night in Manhattan. Why that one?

"I refuse to believe it was just coincidence," he says. "God has been arranging encounters in human history since the beginning of time, and it's no stretch for me to imagine that He could reach into a coffee shop in Manhattan and turn an ordinary gig into a revival."

:: :: ::

GOD WINKS ON THE LIVING

When we suffer deeply from the loss of someone we love dearly, God's winks are messages to the living, not to those who have gone ahead.

At the time, it is difficult to understand—you hurt to the core, you wonder how you can possibly continue on, you are frightened by the uncertainty of living without this special person in your life. But God is putting His hand on your shoulder, consoling you, letting you know that our existence is not a continuum but a circle, and connections to loved ones are never lost.

Every godwink is another reminder—another small, still message from God—that everything is going to be okay. Someday you will see everything from His perspective, and you'll understand. Your loved one has graduated. Someday you will too. We all graduate, one way or the other.

CHAPTER FOUR

GOD WINKS ON COMFORT

There comes a time—I don't care how tough you think you are—when we all just need a hug.

It could be a day when the bottom falls out of your plans like a soggy cardboard box unceremoniously spilling its contents on the floor.

It could be a day when the pink slip you dreaded is in the envelope.

It could be a day when weariness and disappointment just bring you to tears.

We all have those days. We feel unwanted, unworthy, or unloved.

Have you ever noticed that's often the time when a little

bright experience bounces into your day? Just there for the enjoying, for the brightening, to help you feel like you are worthy, wanted, and not alone?

See if some of the following stories replicate your own experiences of receiving godwinks of comfort at just the right moment and for no other purpose than to deliver you a personal heavenly hug.

MOMMY IN RED

"You can never wear red, because you've got red hair," taunted her classmate, sounding like Lucy in the Charlie Brown cartoons.

Bethany Skillen wondered how the mean-spirited words of an eleven-year-old, spoken years before, could have such an impact upon her. Yet here she was, a young wife and mother, thirty years old, still haunted by the snotty comments of a sixth-grade classmate.

She was feeling defiant. She could wear red if she wanted to!

She needed to feel defiant. Two days ago she had been crushed.

Having a second child quite so soon didn't sound like a good idea at first. Jamie was still studying for his PhD at Cornell, and the income of a teaching assistant just wasn't enough. But once the doctor confirmed the pregnancy, Bethany and Jamie were elated. She enthusiastically started telling everyone.

When Bethany was pregnant with Sam, now one-and-a-half, she heeded the advice that you shouldn't mention your condition to others for the first thirteen weeks because that's when most miscarriages occur. But Sam was born without a hitch, and this time she wanted people to know.

When she learned that she had miscarried her baby, it was devastating.

She cried for two days, feeling such a terrible sense of mourning. Her baby had died before she could get to know it, hold it, love it.

Bethany had told her mom—her best friend—no, she didn't have to make that six-hour trip from Martha's Vineyard to Ithaca to be with her. Bethany thought she could handle this on her own, but truth be known, she really wanted her mom's hug.

Now it was time to pull herself together. "I've got to get out," she said.

Bethany and little Sam headed for the Target store. She didn't have much money—$20 and some change, left over from a Christmas gift. She was strolling the aisles, just looking.

Then it struck her.

"I can wear red if I want to!"

In fact, what she'd always wanted was a pair of red shoes. Yeah . . . red Mary Janes . . . the kind she once saw Dorothy wearing in *The Wizard of Oz*. Of course, fat chance she could find red Mary Janes in her size for about twenty bucks.

> Hope is the feeling that the feeling you have isn't permanent.[1]
>
> —JEAN KERR

Bethany turned the corner and almost instantly encountered her blessing. There, on a markdown table, her eyes focused on a pair of red shoes—Mary Janes—in her size!

Quickly she slipped off her shoes and tried on the red ones.

Ahh . . . this must be how Cinderella felt, she thought. *They fit perfectly.*

Oh, oh . . . check the price.

Bethany's mouth opened involuntarily.

The price was $21.50. But that wasn't what floored her. Boldly imprinted on the inside of the beautiful red shoes was the designer name: Bethany.

That morning, she had desperately wanted a hug from her mother. Instead, she'd gotten a hug from her Father. God winked at her in a moment of lonely grieving by delivering a small miracle of comfort.

Red shoes with her own name inside.

:: :: ::

LITTLE CONNECTIONS, BIG LIFT

Making sense out of senseless things is one of the tasks we are all called on to perform from time to time.

When a little godwink shows up serendipitously in your life, like Bethany's red shoes, try to resist your left brain's demand for rational reasoning—just accept it as a little message from above, saying: "Hey kid, everything is going to be okay."

A PLACE IN THE VILLAGE

Ellen Pall's mother died young.

It was young for both of them.

Her mother, Josephine Blatt Pall, was forty-five when a rare form of anemia sadly took her life.

Ellen was only seven.

Memories of her mother were elusive. Ellen knew her mother had been an artist, a writer, and thought of herself as a Bostonian, which is where Josephine grew up. Truth be known, Ellen deeply wished she'd known her mother more.

Ellen was raised by her father, stepmother, and Steffi, her

older sister by nine years. Ellen studied English and French at the University of California at Santa Barbara and moved to New York in 1984. She already had written eight books and was to become a prolific author of mysteries, literary novels, and a frequent contributor to the *New York Times*.

As a new New Yorker, Ellen was thrilled to write to her sister, Steffi, about a lovely apartment she had found in Greenwich Village—a narrow, four-story building at 288 West 12th Street.

"It's covered with ivy and has a little plaque on the front saying it was built in 1848," she wrote. "You would love it."

Steffi wrote back, recalling that their mother had once lived in Greenwich Village, too, before they were born.

"I'll get in touch with Mother's old friend, Debbie Sankey, and find out where," said Steffi.

Ellen set about turning the little apartment into a home. There was a living room with a fireplace, a skylight in the kitchen, and one window looked into a courtyard.

Before long, Steffi excitedly telephoned with a note in hand: "Listen to this! Debbie Sankey wrote that she was Mother's roommate in 1938, and she says they had an apartment on West 12th Street."

Debbie said that she couldn't be sure of the street number, but it was a narrow building across the street from a restaurant, the Beatrice Inn.

"I seem to have the number 288 West 12th in my head," Debbie wrote. Ellen was flabbergasted. Could it be that forty-six years apart, she and her mother had rented an apartment in the same tiny New York City building?

Hanging up with her sister, Ellen rushed to a carton of her mother's old papers and memorabilia that she had kept. She pawed through penny postcards, letters on yellowing paper, and various unpublished writings.

Then her fingers grasped exactly what she was looking for—confirmation—a poem with her mother's name and address on the cover sheet: "Jo Blatt, 288 W. 12th St."

Unbelievable, she thought, scribbling her innermost feelings into her journal on the night of the great discovery: "I got chills and tears and tremors. It can't be mere coincidence, yet it's unlikely to be anything else."

Whatever the cause of the mystery, she concluded: "It's one of those rare circumstances that seem to give life some incontrovertible order, and the fact that my mother opened these doors, passed by this railing, pleases me very much."

By this extraordinary godwink, she was "comforted and reassured that she had landed in the right place."

Oh yes! Across the street, the Beatrice Inn was still open for business. Think of it . . . she had dined where her mother had surely dined.

NATALIE'S PARIS

"Daddy, I'm not looking up people I've never met," said Natalie.

"Just look," said her father, Ara Garibian, excited that his college-aged daughter was spending a semester in Paris. He pointed to an old black-and-white photo, trimmed in white, ragged edges, glued into a tattered photo album.

"These little girls would be grown by now," he continued unabashed, advising his daughter that there might be family members living in France.

"First of all, Daddy, I'm too shy to go knocking on people's doors. Secondly, I'm going there to study."

It turned out that Natalie's first two months in Paris were nothing like she expected. She was overwhelmed with the challenges of language and the loneliness for home. She wrestled with the benefits of quitting, while fearing the shame of failure.

One Sunday morning she was drawn to a quaint Armenian church, tucked among the boutiques on a famous Parisian boulevard. Perhaps being among people who spoke her first language, Armenian, would make her feel less homesick.

She took a seat out of the way, on a chair that was set at the end of a pew. But she was soon to discover that everyone spoke French. *Still out of place,* she thought, as the service wound on and on. She looked around, considering the option of getting up and slipping out early. *Not a good idea . . . too disturbing.*

Going down the aisle, an older woman looking for a seat passed Natalie. As she returned up the aisle, several people spoke to her in French, offering a seat. She ignored them.

As she approached, Natalie stood and spoke to her in Armenian.

"Would you like to sit down?"

The woman nodded and Natalie withdrew nearby, tucking herself under a stone archway.

The service continued.

Natalie caught the old woman glancing at her.

Intermittently, Natalie stole looks back. She studied the character of the woman's countenance. She admired that the woman held to the old customs of the church, covering her head with a lace scarf. Most younger people, including herself, were not doing that.

As parishioners solemnly filed to the front of the church for communion, the old woman turned to Natalie.

"You're not from here, are you?" she asked in Armenian.

"No. How did you know?" whispered Natalie.

"You spoke to me in Armenian. I don't speak French. Where are you from?"

"Florida," smiled Natalie.

"Florida . . . we have family there," brightened the old woman, "nephews—Sarkis and Dikran . . ."

Suddenly Natalie knew what she was going to say. She blurted out, "Ara!"

"Yes . . . Ara," said the old woman, her eyes widening.

"That's my dad!"

"I knew you were someone special," said the woman, her face wrinkling joyfully, her eyes welling.

They were unaware they had been speaking so loudly. People in front were turning to shush them. But others had been listening and now they, too, were stifling tears.

"I've been looking for your father for a long, long time," said the woman. "I'm your Aunt Arev. Before your father could find his way to America, he stayed with me in Aleppo, Syria . . . but we never knew what happened to him."

After church, Natalie walked her great aunt to the bus stop. She promised to come to dinner that evening to meet Aunt Arev's daughters, two of the little girls in the black-and-white photo, now grown.

Then she rushed to a pay phone and hurriedly dialed home.

"Daddy! You'll never guess what happened!"

She couldn't wait to tell him Auntie Arev's last words uttered in disbelief in Armenian.

"It's God's work. It's all God's work."

You've Been There

You've been in Natalie's shoes at one time or another. In a new environment—a different school or job—where you felt out of place and uncomfortable. You wanted to flee to a place of greater familiarity and comfort. Yet you were held there by a sense of obligation or possible embarrassment if you were to leave.

> I will fear no evil; for You *are* with me; Your rod and Your staff, they comfort me.
>
> —Psalm 23:4 NKJV

God senses these moments in your life. And if you are open to receiving them, He sends you messages of reassurance—godwinks—designed to bring you hugs of comfort at those times of uncertainty.

SAM'S JAM

Sammy was a cute little mutt. Kind of a skinny Westie, I think.

I would see Sammy excitedly pulling on his owner's leash—glad to be out of the New York apartment where he lived on East 79th Street—to take his morning walk.

As I waited to put my son on the school bus, I'd first say hello to Sammy and then to his owner, Richard Temtchine.

Sammy's name was pronounced "Sammy." Richard's name was pronounced "Ree-chard." He was French—an independent film producer. I enjoyed his musical, French accented "Good morning" almost as much as seeing Sammy trying to pull this grown man onto the street faster than he wanted to go.

As was the case every day, Sammy went jogging in Central Park with Richard. They were running quite some distance from home, at 109th Street. Because Richard knew Sammy always stayed very close to him, particularly in strange places, he took Sammy off his leash. Ahhh. This was always a treat for Sammy. The freedom to scamper! But not too far. Oh no, he'd stay close to Richard.

What no one anticipated was a sudden appearance by the tough creature that controlled that area of Central Park: a huge Doberman, the kind Disney would cast as the typical "bad-guy" dog. As the Doberman burst from the shadows—snarling, barking, and baring teeth, demanding to know why this skinny little dog was in his territory—Sammy did exactly what you or I would have done. He bolted. He ran and ran and ran. He had no idea where he was going because, as a city dog, he generally went to places only when on his owner's leash. The only territory Sammy was familiar with was the block or two near Richard's 79th Street apartment.

Richard was heartsick. He looked everywhere. He dreaded

going home, facing his wife, Jill, with the terrible news that Sammy was lost. Worse was the prospect of telling their nine-year-old daughter, Chloe, when she returned from school.

"But he has a name tag," said Jill in a voice choked with emotion. "Perhaps somebody will find him and call us."

Richard shrugged. The prospects of someone stopping and looking at Sammy's collar just seemed improbable at the time.

But he had to take action. He enlisted friends and laid out assignments for each person to search a specific quadrant of Central Park. They would rendezvous back at the apartment, hopefully, with good news before Chloe got home at 3:00 P.M.

The searchers spread out. They looked and looked. Up one pathway of the park and down another, they called out "Sammy, Sammy!" By 2:45 P.M., the searchers reassembled at the apartment, each bearing a dejected countenance and with nothing to report.

The housekeeper had left a note. Someone had called.

Richard dialed the phone.

"Bonjour . . ." answered an operator.

"I'm sorreee, I have the wrong number," said Richard, thinking he had dialed the wrong number. He dialed again.

"Bonjour . . ." answered the operator again.

"Hello," said Richard, hesitantly. "Someone left this number to call. My name is Richard Temtchine."

"Oui, monsieur," said the operator, "these ees the French Embassy. Your leetle puppy has come to visit us. He ees in our garden, right now. And we noticed a tag weese your number."

A burst of joy!

Somehow little Sammy traveled thirty New York City blocks and came to rest at a place he'd never visited before—the French Embassy. Sammy was thereby dubbed: "The First True Bilingual Dog" of New York.

:: :: ::

THE HUG

As a child, you found refuge from things that were frightening, uncertain, or sad, by crawling into your mom or dad's lap and receiving a warm, strong hug. You were wrapped with a love that dissolved everything scary—you were safe and at peace.

Now as a grown-up, hugs come in a different form. There may be someone in your life who hugs you in a special way— you feel a surge of amalgamated energy that could be attributed only to the presence of God. And then there are the small miracles—the baffling, unbelievable experiences called god-winks—sending you hugs directly from Him.

CHAPTER FIVE

GOD WINKS ON PRAYER

Prayer is a powerful fact of life—and I use the word *fact* purposely.

We believers know that from personal experience.

If you have prayed for a healing miracle—if doctors have told you that you or someone you love has little or no chance to live, and then following prayer, you witness the awesome, intervening power of God to pull you or that person from the brink of death—you know that prayer is *fact*.

If you are at the edge of everything falling apart—you're totally broke, all the cards are stacked against you, you're flat on your face at the bottom, people don't want to be around you, and bankruptcy or leaping from the nearest bridge seems to be the only answer—and then out of the blue, you get relief, or a fervent prayer has been answered—*that* is a *factual* experience in your life.

Of course, the world is full of doubters. If you are one of them, you just haven't yet had the firsthand experience of so many believers. Someday you will be up against a wall like others in this chapter, and God will make Himself known to you at that time. Then and there, prayer will become a *fact* of life in *your* life.

And keep this in mind: God is a God of second chances.

ASKING FOR A SECOND CHANCE

"Hold on Mac . . . I'm not going to leave you!" shouted Gerry, the younger of the two men struggling to keep their heads above water.

"I'm cold . . . I don't think I can hold on any longer," shivered Mac, his lips blue from the cold December waters.

"Just keep hanging on to that stick!" shouted Gerry, trying desperately to believe his own words. "It'll be light soon . . . somebody will see us."

Gerry Ponson, his older friend, Mac Ansespy, and Mac's black Labrador retriever had left shore at 5:00 AM to cross the three-mile bay near New Orleans to their favorite duck-hunting spot. The forecast had called for nasty weather, yet they thought if they got their seventeen-foot open-bay boat across early enough, they could make it. But reaching the center of the bay, the waters became increasingly choppy as a north-wester charged suddenly into the channel and bore down upon them, tossing their craft like a toy.

When seawater splashed over them, Mac momentarily took his hands from the steering wheel to clean his glasses. In that instant, the rough waters seized the direction of the boat, causing it to be sideways in the waves.

"Turn the boat, turn the boat!" Gerry shouted, but it was too late. A huge wave crashed in on them, instantly filling their boat, causing it to sink in eight feet of water.

One of the few items in the craft that Gerry could grab was a ten-foot push pole used for pushing a boat through shallow waters. By plunging the stick into the mud and standing on the gunnels of the boat, they could just keep their heads above water. "Grab that pole, Mac, and hold on," Gerry repeated to his friend.

In a quick assessment, Gerry knew Mac was in no shape to swim to shore. Besides, until the sun came up, they might be swimming in circles. He also considered leaving Mac and swimming for help. But even if he made it ashore, it was five miles to the nearest phone. And Mac couldn't survive on his own. No . . . he'd wait . . . maybe a boat would come up the channel.

Alternately, Gerry would prop up Mac, then grab the dog by the collar and help him stay afloat for a few minutes. Finally, Gerry made a decision. He told the dog to go.

"Where's Booga?" gasped Mac, disoriented after two hours in the water, looking for his champion black Lab.

"I tol' him to git. I can save you, Mac, but I can't save your dog."

In his heart he knew the dog would never make it. A mile-and-a-half across the channel in those nasty waters would be too much for any creature.

Gerry's constant movement was staving off hypothermia while Mac's body temperature plunged dangerously low, causing a shutdown of body functions in the frigid waters and biting wind.

"I'm cold, Gerry . . . I can't hold on any longer," Mac panted, mentally letting go as well.

"Hold on, Mac. Somebody'll come."

Gerry didn't really believe that.

He didn't believe in anything. He'd been a heathen all his adult life. There were times as a kid when he sort of allowed that God existed, but as an adult he was a self-described "drinkin', cheatin' heathen, looking for love in all the wrong places."

His sister had tried. She tried to talk to him about God, but he'd called her a fruitcake—and worse—told her to "get her blankety-blank outta his house."

Smash!

A wave drenched him.

"Hold on, Mac!"

Maybe he should have listened to her. His girlfriend, Shannon, too . . . she was a believer. She didn't press him like his sister had . . . gave him his space . . . but he knew she wished he'd come on board with the Lord.

"I can't hold on anymore," said Mac, weaker now.

Smash. Another wave.

"Yes, you can! Hold on," encouraged Gerry, trying to buy his own baloney, but this was bad. Really bad. Inside his head he was saying, *We're gonna die out here. Nobody's comin' . . . we're gonna die.*

Gerry lifted his eyes toward the sky, unsure of how to say what he was going to say. "God . . . if you hear me . . . please, please send us a boat. Send us a boat, God. Please save us."

His own words startled him . . . he couldn't believe what he had just said.

Then—not two minutes later—he couldn't believe what his eyes were seeing.

"Mac . . . I see something!"

Through the morning mist Gerry could see the shadows of a cross . . . the mast of a boat coming through the channel. Through the haze he started to make it out . . . a big boat . . . probably seventy-five feet long.

"They'll see us, Mac. Hold on to me!" he shouted, pulling the push pole from the mud, attaching a shirt to one end, waving it frantically in the air.

"Over here!" he shouted repeatedly.

Doubtful thoughts rushed through his mind. Would they see them—just a blob in rough waters? Would somebody on that boat be looking off to the south, at just the right moment, to see somebody where they shouldn't be, off in the distance waving a shirt on a pole?

"Make 'em see us, God!" shouted Gerry, now in-for-a-penny-in-for-a-pound with the Lord.

"Mac . . . I think they see us! They've stopped! But that big boat can't get over here. It's not deep enough."

Then Gerry saw that someone had leaped from the boat and was swimming toward them.

"They're coming, Mac, hold on."

A man told Mac to lie on his back, and he'd pull him the hundred yards or so to the boat. On his own, Gerry began swimming to safety. It hadn't dawned on him yet that within moments of asking for help from the Almighty, the boat actually showed up. But the moment Gerry saw the name of the boat, it struck him—like a ton of bricks. He knew right then and there that God had heard his pleading prayer and had saved him.

The boat's name was *Second Chance*.

On board the boat, he met the owners—a husband and wife. It was Karen who had spotted them, and her husband, Bimbo, who had jumped in to rescue Mac. They gave them some dry clothes and tried to get them warm. But Mac was not doing so well. He complained of chest pains.

As Karen and Bimbo comforted Mac, Gerry picked up the radio and quickly shouted "Mayday, Mayday!"

A voice cracked over the radio. It was the Coast Guard. They said to hold on. Soon a flapping sound indicated that a medevac chopper had arrived, and it was lowering a medic who would grasp Mac in a sling and pull him up.

It was an emergency. They couldn't take the time to also lift Gerry into the chopper. But Bimbo and Karen let Gerry ashore at the earliest opportunity. Bimbo arranged for his brother to meet them and to give Gerry a lift to his pickup truck to drive to the hospital to check on Mac.

On the drive to the hospital, the power of what had happened that day raced through Gerry's mind—the near-death tragedy and the miracle rescue. A flood of tears were triggered as Gerry pulled to the side of the road. He placed his head in his arms on the steering wheel and thanked the Almighty.

"Did you find Booga?" muttered Mac from his hospital bed.

Gerry sadly shook his head, knowing that the dog couldn't have made it. But he promised his friend he would try to find Booga and give him a good burial.

"He's a world-class champion," uttered Mac.

"I know," said Gerry, remembering how proudly Mac had announced that his black Labrador retriever, Booga, was voted third in the nation in his class.

> Here I am! I stand at the door and knock. If you hear my voice and open the door, I will come in.
>
> —REVELATION 3:20 NCV

Later that day, Gerry borrowed a boat to search the marshy shoreline for any sign of Booga even though he knew it was a hopeless task.

"Woof."

"Booga! Is that you?"

Tears again welled up in Gerry's eyes. He couldn't believe that God was offering second chances twice in one day! There was Booga, just waiting to be rescued from the desolate marsh.

"'Hey, where ya been?' that's what Booga was sayin' to me," smiled Gerry later.

Gerry Ponson experienced a major transformation in his life. It was emblazoned on his heart and mind that a boat named *Second Chance* had been delivered to him through prayer, just as he was giving up all hope. Gerry committed himself to serving his Maker for the rest of his life. He's been a street preacher ever since.

Don't try to convince Gerry that prayer is not "fact" . . . he knows differently!

Eleven days after he was lifted from those cold waters in the bay, Gerry made things right with Shannon. Wanting to start the new year with a clean slate, he asked her to marry him—on December 30th. After all, he'd already been given an incredible godwink—a second chance.

Gerry came to realize that being seen through the haze by someone on that boat, in such rough waters, was not all of it—

> You call out to God for help and he helps—he's a good Father that way.
>
> —1 PETER 1:17
> THE MESSAGE

that boat was not even supposed to be there. Bimbo told Gerry that the impending storm had altered the tides, causing them to delay their crossing of the bay the night before. By all rights, they should have gone the long way into the Gulf of Mexico. What an even more spectacular wink from God that the boat named *Second Chance* showed up where it did!

EVIDENCE

Scientific studies to clinically confirm the efficacy of prayer have doubled in the past decade—encouraging news for those of us who have always known the power of prayer.

Dr. Mitchell Krucoff, a cardiologist at Duke University, randomly selected 150 heart patients and placed them into five groups for a pilot research project. One group received standard cardiac care. Three others received treatments from a bedside therapist described as imagery, stress relaxation, and touch therapy. A final group received distant "off-site intercessory prayer."

Those in the prayer therapy group improved by more than 50 percent. "There may be a benefit to these therapies," said Dr. Krucoff, cautiously optimistic. He has subsequently expanded the study to fifteen hundred patients.[1]

At St. Luke's Hospital in Kansas City, cardiac researcher William Harris, PhD, also found positive results from a study of intercessory or distant prayer on one thousand heart patients with prior cardiac conditions of a serious nature.

They were randomly assigned to two groups: Without knowing it, half received daily prayer for two weeks, half had no prayer. Those who received prayer fared 11 percent better.[2]

In a similar study, at San Francisco General Hospital in 1988, patients who received prayer were able to leave the hospital sooner.[3]

Dr. Harold Koenig, Duke's associate professor of medicine and psychiatry, stated that some twelve hundred studies on the effects of prayer and health were conducted at such universities as Duke, Dartmouth, and Yale. These were some of the results published in his book *Handbook of Religion and Health*.[4]

Hospitalized people who attended church regularly had an average stay three times shorter than people who didn't.

Heart patients who participated in religion were 14 percent more likely to live following surgery than those who didn't.

The elderly who attended church regularly were 50 percent less likely to suffer strokes than those who didn't go to church.

In Israel, religious people were 40 percent less likely to die from cardiovascular disease and cancer than those who weren't religious.

Dr. Koenig was also quoted in *USA Today* as saying, "Healthy senior citizens who said they rarely or never prayed ran about a 50 percent greater risk of dying" from their cardiac condition.[5]

Have I made my point? The efficacy of prayer is *fact*.

A WINK IN WICHITA

Janine leaned against the kitchen counter, sobbing quietly. Her boys were in the next room, and she didn't want them to hear.

In a depressed daze, she kept opening and closing the refrigerator, then the cabinet doors, hoping to find something she'd somehow missed for the kids to eat. Nothing—not even a bag of rice.

Her ex-husband hadn't sent a support check in two years. No use expecting anything from him. She was on her own.

It had been thirty days since Raytheon Aircraft laid her off, and she couldn't think straight. She couldn't find a solution to her problem. Couldn't imagine how she could buy groceries or make the house payment before the next unemployment check would arrive.

The boys' laughter rose from the den. *How long would it be before they had nothing to laugh about,* she wondered.

She was scared. With the downturn in the airline industry after September 11, 2001, she was just one of eleven thousand workers who'd lost aviation-related jobs in Wichita. Without special skills, she wouldn't be on anyone's list to rehire.

With a quiet sigh, Janine closed her eyes. Her lips moved ever so slightly with her prayer of desperation.

The doorbell rang—or tried to—giving off its annoying buzz. Something was wrong with it, but like the peeling paint on the house, the car that leaked oil, and the washing machine that filled only halfway, it was just one more unfixable problem way down her list of priorities.

Janine hastily wiped her reddened eyes with a damp paper towel and peered through the front door glass. She recognized the man on her front stoop. He wasn't a friend, just an acquaintance from church. She hadn't spoken to him in years.

Why was he here now, standing on her porch at five thirty in the evening?

"Hi, Steve," Janine greeted, surprised that she'd remembered his first name. "Come on in."

As he stepped into the hallway, he looked a bit surprised himself even to be there.

"Janine, you'll never guess why I'm here. I hope you don't

think I'm crazy, but God wouldn't let me go home tonight."

Janine just looked at him.

"He wouldn't let me go home until I wrote you a check."

Janine's mouth fell open. A check?

"All day long, you were on my mind," he continued, "and God was telling me you needed a lift. Will you take this?" In his outstretched hand was a folded check.

Janine mutely looked at the check for $800, then back to Steve—stunned by his generosity and even more by God's message to her.

"Thank you," she whispered.

Her heart lifted, knowing she wasn't so alone after all. Now she could buy groceries and even get the boys a treat.

"You don't have to pay me back," Steve said hastily. "It's a gift, and I want you to call if you need more later."

"Thank you," she repeated, too choked up to speak, but this time with her face uplifted to God.

SOMEBODY KNOWS THE TROUBLE I'VE SEEN

I wonder how many readers have been in Janine's situation: downsized, pummeled by unexpected trouble, or otherwise left in a state of despair, up against the proverbial wall, staring at a checking account that was incapable of paying the rent and putting food on the table.

In reviewing those dark times, was it your faith and the power of prayer that pulled you through?

EXPECTING THE UNEXPECTED

By trade Mary Haise was an accountant. Numbers came easy for her.

Still, she was puzzled by one aspect of the church donor form. She got the part about tithing a certain amount to the church each week. Surely the church board needed to know how much they could expect she would commit over the course of the year. It was the little box at the bottom that was new to her. It said, "Check here to tithe unexpected income."

> The effectual fervent prayer of a righteous man availeth much.
>
> —JAMES 5:16 KJV

Unexpected income?

Oh, she got it. If she won the lottery, she would commit to give the church its fair share . . . normally 10 percent.

Well, why not? she thought. If she were to come into a nice chunk of "unexpected" cash, why shouldn't God get His fair share?

In a bold stroke, she placed a check mark in the little box. On her drive home, Mary began thinking about the prospects of "unexpected income." How *much*, for instance. How much income would she like to have turn up on her doorstep?

How about fifty grand?

Yeah . . . fifty thousand dollars . . . that would be nice right about now, with the crunch her finances had been in lately. She could finally buy that condo she had been dreaming about as a retirement home.

> If you expect the worst, you get the worst. And if you expect the best, you will get the best.[6]
>
> —NORMAN VINCENT PEALE

Pulling into her driveway, Mary made a strong, affirmative statement.

"Okay God, I am asking you for fifty thousand dollars in 'unexpected income.'"

Exactly three days later, Mary's godwink arrived.

Ripping through her daily stack of mail, Mary opened a routine statement from her brokerage firm. Its contents shocked her.

"Oh!" she gasped, then audibly inhaling, stared wide-eyed at the statement.

The brokers reported that stock, which had been in her

father's will, previously worth only pennies, had suddenly exploded. The paper in front of her reported a value of $50,000.

Exactly.

Mary felt gratitude and euphoria the following Sunday when she wrote a check for $5000, fulfilling her 10 percent promise. She slipped it into the offering basket at church, laughing to herself as she wrote at the bottom, "tithing of unexpected income."

But confirmation that God is truly the author of all blessings came during the service when Pastor Victoria Etchemendy announced that the church building fund was running short.

"We need an additional $5000 for our Sunday school space," said Victoria, not yet aware of Mary's envelope in the offering.

Perhaps it was Mary's imagination, but that morning everything around her seemed to shine with an unusual brightness.

∷ ∷ ∷

GOD IS ALWAYS LISTENING

I have found that God hears our prayers even if He doesn't answer them in the way we expect or on our timetables. In Mary's case, her prayer may have seemed like a whimsical request, but as she later described it, "I immediately felt a shift inside, almost a physical thing, that went really deep on a trust level." God demonstrated that He *was* listening—that He really knew the desires of her heart.

Mary's experience brings me back to something I wrote earlier—that once, even while I was complaining, God still listened and answered my prayer.

Though I have come to understand that, in most cases, prayer works best when we *expect* God to answer our prayers, following are two stories about the recipients of answered prayer who were actually surprised by the outcomes.

A PRAYER OF REUNION

Betty and Andy sat on the couch, shoulder to shoulder, reminiscing over the decades as they turned the pages of the family photo album. Two of the oldest photographs dated from the 1940s—a young soldier, fresh-faced and sharply dressed, at a kitchen table next to a chubby, dimpled baby in a high chair. The next photo showed the baby boy on his rocking horse.

In the pages that followed, an older boy with the same dimpled chin smiled at the camera on trips to the lake, at picnics with cousins, and from behind glowing birthday cakes. The man in the uniform—the baby's father—was no longer in any of those photos.

"Wouldn't it be nice to know whatever happened to your dad?" Betty mused.

Andy didn't answer.

Long ago, he'd put that question to rest. He'd assumed—or maybe he'd been told—that his real father was dead. Killed in a car accident. But he'd never heard the details, never seen the grave.

A nagging doubt persisted about his father. But when he asked his mother, she'd simply reply, "Don't ask me." So he stopped asking.

For almost sixty years, he tried not to think about his story. It was the story of his life, but with crucial pages ripped away.

Betty decided to pray about it. She clasped her hands and bowed her head.

"Dear God, help my husband learn the identity of his father."

Twelve hundred miles away, an old man's fingers picked up a curled photo and looked at his baby son. The edges of the photo were worn thin. For fifty-eight years, instead of holding his son, two photos were all he had to hold. Their stained and torn edges showed the love they'd received, poor substitutes for the child himself.

"Take a good look at this kid," his wife Mildred had said

sharply when she took their baby and slammed the door, back in 1946. "It'll be the last time you ever see him."

It was a wartime romance that ended when the war ended.

George Henderson didn't believe her at first, thinking the threat was just angry words of a failed marriage. But she was right. He was never able to find her or his son after that. Eventually he moved back to his home state of Kansas.

George remarried later on and moved to Topeka, where he'd grown up. But he never stopped looking, wondering, wishing he could find his son.

"I wish I knew where Andy was," he would say.

Relatives and friends pitched in from time to time with phone calls and Internet searches. One fruitless search after another.

One day in 2003, Topeka's water clerk, Gloria Hollister, learned from a nephew that George had a long lost son—his only child—and heard about George's futile search over the years.

Gloria had always liked George and enjoyed chatting with him when he came into City Hall to pay his water bill. She'd had some success tracing her own family history, so she decided to put her skills to work.

With the initial sleuthing, Gloria found that George's child was still alive. His last name was no longer Henderson but

Kellogg. Knowing that George's first wife was originally from Nevada, she searched for "Kellogg" in that state.

Jackpot! Ten names downloaded onto her screen. Andy Kellogg, Las Vegas, Nevada, was the last name on the list.

Gloria excitedly called George's nephew and told him that perhaps George's son was alive. She gave him the phone number for Andy Kellogg.

But wasn't it too late?

George's wife and relatives were worried. Fifty-eight years had passed. George was eighty-seven. It was crazy to open up a Pandora's box of potential ill feeling and anger. What if his son wanted nothing to do with him? George's circle of friends and relatives cautioned: "He might say, 'You're a stranger. I don't know you.'"

"I'll accept that," George said calmly.

A relative in Nevada made the first contact, dialing Andy Kellogg in Las Vegas. But the voice of this Andy was too young. It turned out to be Andy Kellogg's son, also named Andy, who gladly provided his dad's unlisted telephone number.

After hanging up, the younger Andy Kellogg called his father. "Dad, I've got a grandpa!" he shouted into the phone.

His father was perplexed. "What are you talking about?"

"Your dad is alive!"

Andy Kellogg hung up the phone in a daze, and looked over

at Betty.

"Didn't you just ask me, not two weeks ago, what had happened to my dad?"

She nodded. "I remember."

"And prayed about it?"

She nodded again.

"Well, your prayer has been answered. He's alive. He's going to call me."

A few days later, the call came, the tears flowed, and when George and Andy finally met in a tearful reunion at the Topeka Airport, father and son found their similarities bridged the decades with almost no effort on their parts.

"It was like we had known each other a long time," Andy said.

"When you wait that long, you just don't think it's going to happen," George marveled.

Andy and Betty met dozens of family members, even some of the people whose names were listed in Andy's baby book—people who'd given him gifts at his birth.

"I like this family. It's just like we have known each other all our lives!" Andy marveled.

> Dreams come true; without that possibility, nature would not incite us to have them.[7]
>
> —JOHN UPDIKE

Thanks to a Godwink Link—the loving help offered by an astute and caring town clerk—a father and son were reunited after fifty-eight years, just two weeks after a wife's prayer was lifted up to God.

At the Henderson and Kellogg homes are new photos in the family albums, the kinds that families cherish—photos of a father and son, arms wrapped around each other, beaming with love and contentment.

A FAN OF POWER

The air was still. The heat was stifling.

Bad enough that it was the fifth day of a mid-nineties heat wave; worse, it was also the fifth day of a power blackout.

The curtains in Denise Fouracres's wide-open kitchen window hadn't moved a millimeter. The fan on the table sat motionless, like a bad joke.

Mother of three boys and one on the way, Denise was at wit's end.

Luke, her three-year-old, was unusually crabby, becoming more so each time he fruitlessly pushed the button on the nonworking fan.

"Popsicle, Mommy," said Luke, wiping his eyes.

"Sorry, baby, Mommy doesn't have any more popsicles. Everything is gone."

"Kool-Aid."

"Sorry, baby."

"Water."

Hugging her three-year-old while expelling a tired breath, Denise slowly shook her head.

> God is the source of all energy. Energy in the universe, atomic energy, electrical energy, and spiritual energy. The Bible emphasizes this point: "He giveth power to the faint."[8]
>
> —NORMAN VINCENT PEALE

"I know baby . . . you're thirsty and hot. But the power's been out for five days and there's no water and nothing in the fridge."

Luke let out a frustrated whine.

In the small town north of Detroit, it was not unusual for a transformer to blow out. But five days? In this heat?

Another disgruntled sound emerged from Luke as he ineffectively and repeatedly struck the fan switch.

Denise sat down, lifted Luke to her lap, and said: "Let's pray about it, Honey, let's ask Jesus to help us."

"Lord, we ask that you bring us relief . . . "

GOD WINKS ON PRAYER

"And turn the fan on!" chimed Luke.

At that very moment . . . the fan began slowly to turn. Gathering speed, a breeze lifted Luke's hair as his eyes widened and his mouth dropped open.

"We should of asked Him yesterday!" exclaimed Luke.

Denise smiled and hugged him, almost startled by the other strange sounds—the TV coming on in the living room, the refrigerator humming, and of course, the rattling of a long dormant fan!

She was also pleased that this small godwink would give her child long-lasting evidence of the power from above. That was confirmed as little Luke dashed out the door to tell the news to his friend across the street where electric power had not yet been restored.

"All you have to do is ask Jesus," she heard him advise the neighbor.

Prayer Works

Repeating myself—*I have learned that prayer works.*

Time and time again Louise and I have found our prayers answered. In fact, I am hard pressed to think of a time they weren't.

A dear aunt was given a 10 percent chance of survival. We and others prayed. Today, she's the picture of good health.

< 117 >

Louise's son, Dan, was hospitalized with a mysterious, life-threatening illness. We prayed. He's totally well.

When our home was being built, the costs skyrocketed—twice the estimate. We were both without income sufficient to extend the construction loan, so we prayed. God answered with a phone call to Louise for a job that produced enough income to get back on track and complete our home.

In an earlier book, I wrote about the power of prayer when my son, Grant, was born in cardiac arrest. His tiny lungs had filled with meconium, his own body waste, and he was without oxygen for an undetermined amount of time. There was little hope, said the doctors, and should he survive, he would be a vegetable.

> Get down on your knees and thank God you are still on your feet.[9]
> —IRISH PROVERB

Around the clock, I prayed over his incubator at the hospital neonatal clinic. Eighteen tubes and wires were connected to his little body. One connected to a meter that registered how much he was breathing on his own, and how much by the machine. It showed 5 percent by him, 95 percent by the apparatus.

Then I witnessed the miracle—the answer to prayer. My son began to shake. I called a nurse.

Calling it a seizure, she ran for a doctor.

I prayed harder.

As I did, I noticed that in one of the tubes—a transparent tube from his lungs—a black substance was moving through. The seizure was casting off the blockage in his baby lungs! And I began to see a change in the meter—his dependence on the machine to produce his breathing began to drop. And two hours later, his forty-eighth hour on earth, the meter indicated fifty-fifty—half of his breathing was on his own.

When I say prayer works—I believe it.

CHAPTER SIX

WINKS ON UNANSWERED PRAYER

My son Grant is now a sweet young man in his twenties, challenged by a residual brain injury, but he is articulate, holds a job, lives with friends of comparable skills, and derives great joy from music. Grant astonishes people with his uncanny ability to sing and remember the lyrics to hundreds and hundreds of songs, particularly country-western music.

One of his favorite performers is Garth Brooks, whose music I've heard scores of times when we travel by car. One song sticks in my mind: "Thank God for Unanswered Prayers."

. . . just because he doesn't answer, doesn't mean he don't care.
Some of God's greatest gifts are unanswered prayers.[1]

Garth Brooks was singing about a man who was somewhere with his wife when he suddenly encountered an old girlfriend. Years before, this was the girl of his dreams. He recalls that every night he prayed about her, asking God to "make her mine."

Now with the clarity of hindsight, it strikes him that she wasn't quite the angel he'd thought she was.

If you're honest with yourself, you'll probably remember that this has happened to you. Your hormones might have been screaming that you'd found Mr. Right—the love of your life—or the girl of your dreams. You prayed that this person would feel the same about you.

Then your prayer wasn't answered. You wondered—or demanded—"Hey, God! Why aren't You listening to me?"

Perhaps another time you were convinced you'd found exactly the right job; you prayed hard for it, and it went to somebody else.

Then there was the time that you wanted something badly —a trip, an apartment, an event. You prayed for it, and it didn't happen.

In each case, your prayer was not answered.

At least not the way *you* had prescribed.

But then, with the clear view of time, you were later able to realize that unanswered prayers are sometimes a real blessing.

You could see how that guy or girl would have been totally wrong for you; how that job would have prevented you from getting another, better job; or how that "something" that didn't happen was actually not in your best interest.

WHY ME, WHY NOW?

So many times the candidate had prayed for good health. But this?

The doctor spoke solemnly: "You've got prostate cancer. We need to treat it right away. I'm sorry, but I'm afraid you'll have to drop everything you're doing—including your run for the Senate."

He stared at his doctor. This wasn't a joke. As outlandish as it seemed, the guy was dead serious.

Why? Why me? were the words screaming inside of him. Alone, he prayed that the doctor was wrong or—if he wasn't—for a miraculous cure. He prayed for the wisdom to know what to do.

In a matter of hours, newsrooms throughout the state received notice that the candidate had scheduled an important news conference.

The media seemed stunned as the candidate looked into

the cameras and said: "We don't always know why these things happen to us in life . . . but in the end . . . they seem to have a way of working themselves out."

That was May 2000.

Sixteen months later, on September 11, 2001, we all found out why—why Rudolph Giuliani was still in the office of mayor of New York City.

> And we know that in all things God works for the good of those who love him, who have been called according to his purpose.
>
> —ROMANS 8:28 NIV

Think about it. If Giuliani had not had prostate cancer and had remained in the race for the Senate against Hillary Clinton, win or lose, he wouldn't have been mayor on 9/11. He would not have been the calming voice for a mourning and shocked nation.

Why hadn't God answered Giuliani's prayers for a healing? Was this an *unanswered* prayer?

Was the prostate cancer God's way of placing Giuliani on the path *He* wanted him on? To fulfill *His* destiny for him?

Giuliani believes so.

"My experience with cancer prepared me for what I had to do after 9/11," he said, "to comfort families during those very difficult days."

ANOTHER PERSPECTIVE

Perhaps Giuliani's terrible news has been matched by something in your own life—something that was delivered to you with the verbal grace of a sledgehammer.

The doctor tried his best to be sympathetic, but telling you the unvarnished truth—partly out of a sense of responsibility and partly out of a fear of being sued—made you wish he'd sugarcoated it. Bottom line, something was wrong with you—something you never expected, something that happens to others, but . . . "why . . . why me?"

Or maybe you associate those words with the day a company bureaucrat wore a dour, downcast look and told you in a rehearsed voice that your position was being "downsized." It probably struck you that corporate America's catchword for "you're fired" only *sounds* better to make *them* feel better.

> Yea, though I
> walk through the
> valley . . .
> —PSALM 23:4 NKJV

Once again, the primordial words surged from your lips: "Why? Why me?"

Or perhaps you heard the brutal message of a spouse—a message not entirely unexpected, but so fearful to face, it was subconsciously shoved way back in your mind. A message that hit you as a surprise even though it wasn't.

WHEN GOD WINKS AT YOU

"I want a divorce."

"What! Why? Why me?" you cried.

We've all had the experience of looking heavenward and asking: "God, why me?"

Terrible things happen to everyone. Sooner or later, we all have to walk through the valley.

In the Bible, David never suggested we could go around the valley or over it. We all have to go *through* it.

But the nice thing about valleys is that there is an end to them. No matter how dark it seems, there's a time when it will end and you'll break into the sunshine. And *that* is the concept you need to hang on to—that there *is* an end to terrible times, to the feelings of loss of control and to the total absence of suitable remedies.

Valleys also have signposts. All along the way God provides winks of reassurance for you to see. Just like on the darkest interstate, a signpost every once in a while is a welcome message of reassurance—a reminder that you're on track, to keep going.

> I'm an old man and have known a great many troubles, but most of them never happened.[2]
>
> —MARK TWAIN

THE SMARTEST MISTAKE

She needed money. A single mom with two kids to raise, Ruth Fertel wasn't making ends meet as a Tulane University lab technician.

The ad in the paper seemed to jump out at her: "For sale, Chris Steak House." A veteran New Orleans restaurateur, Chris Matulich, was selling his business.

"I can do that," said Ruth positively.

That was a big idea. Having experience running a restaurant was *not* something on Ruth's resume.

But . . . she had faith in God. She believed in herself. And she knew that the name *Chris Steak House* had great value. For forty years they'd built up a loyal clientele. All she had to do was keep it going.

So Ruth Fertel mortgaged her house for $18,000 to buy the restaurant. From that day forward, the woman with a degree in chemistry and physics learned restaurant management on the job.

"I don't know whether I was naive or just plain old stupid, but I never thought I would fail," she said, years later. "The hours were terrible, but customers saw how hard I was working, and they wanted me to succeed. Besides, I thought my employees would respect me more if I worked right alongside them, so I did."

For the next ten years her business grew stronger and stronger. They went from selling 35 steaks a day to 250.

Then disaster struck.

Her restaurant burned to the ground.

She owed a large sum of money, so if she didn't reopen right away, she'd be bankrupt. Moreover, being out-of-sight-out-of-mind for any length of time would be deadly for business.

What to do. What to do.

Ruth was in tears when she arrived at her banker's office, hoping he might have an idea.

"Why don't you just reopen in the building you already own down the street?" suggested the banker.

Ruth thought about it. Not a bad idea. She'd purchased the other location nearby for wedding receptions and private parties. But how could she get it ready quickly?

Then a godwink.

"It just so happened that a man who did construction was in the bank at the time," said Ruth. "He said he could get my new location open in a week. And he did."

But just as they were about to move in, Ruth was given more bad news. Her attorney reminded her that the original agreement stipulated that the name *Chris Steak House* could only be used in the original location. By moving to a new address, she could be sued.

Now what to do? She couldn't very well change the name of a business that she'd spent a decade building up, not to mention the untold value of the prior forty years in which the restaurant operated under that name.

Ruth thought about it for a moment. She said a quick prayer.

"I don't have time to do a marketing study on the name, and I can't afford a lawsuit. So just put my name in front. That's it," she said decisively to her attorney and again later that day to her sign maker and menu printer.

They all looked at her blankly.

"Just add my name in front of it," she repeated to them. "Just call it *Ruth's Chris Steak House.*"

It *was* a mouthful. And we're not talking steak.

Almost without missing a beat, Ruth opened in the new location just seven days later.

When her restaurant had burned to the ground, she had looked heavenward and said: "Why, why me, Lord?" Then when she rolled up her sleeves and got to work at solving the problem, a wonderful blessing unfolded—another godwink: the original restaurant only sat sixty people. That caused a

WHEN GOD WINKS AT YOU

two-hour wait to get in, discouraging some potential customers. But the new restaurant—Ruth's Chris Steak House—
seated 160.

"Business just boomed again," said Ruth.

The following year, Ruth started franchising. That's when
she learned that outside of New Orleans the name was a serious liability—people seemed to be continually mispronounc-
ing it: "Ruth's Chrises" or "Chris's
Ruth." One man in San Antonio
called it the stupidest name he'd
ever heard, and only after he was
coaxed in and tasted the steak,
did he change his mind.

> If you want the
> rainbow, you gotta
> put up with the
> rain.[3]
>
> —DOLLY PARTON

Like every other time, Ruth
said a prayer and faced the name
problem head-on. In Baton Rouge, Houston, and Dallas, she
came up with an advertising campaign that said: "We know
we have a funny name, but we have great steaks." Another ad
boldly said: "Our steak is so extraordinary, it needs two
names."

Soon food critics, charmed by the odd name and the self-
deprecating advertising, started writing about the restaurants,
giving Ruth's Chris Steak House topnotch ratings.

Facing the devastation of having her restaurant being

destroyed by fire was one thing. But coming up with that name at the last minute—"That was the smartest mistake I ever made," said Ruth Fertel.

Over the years, Ruth uttered many prayers asking the Lord to help her build her business, but having a fire destroy her restaurant wasn't one of them. Later she could see that the fire was an *unanswered prayer*—it moved her into a larger space and inspired the unique name that we all know today, at nearly ninety Ruth's Chris Steak Houses across America.

RABBIT TO BE OR NOT TO BE

It has been said that my wife, Louise DuArt, is one of the world's best comedic impressionists. (I'd say *the* best, if she'd allow it.) That means she has the remarkable ability to turn on a dime into a hundred different personalities—from Barbara Walters to Judge Judy; Marge Simpson to Kermit the Frog.

Yet strange as it may seem, the opportunity to develop a character for an animated children's television series had somehow eluded her.

You can imagine the thrill when one day she received a call from a casting director at an animation studio.

"Steven Spielberg is doing an animated series for TV, and he's designed a character perfect for you," said the woman. "A rabbit who does impressions."

"Wow. What a prayer answered!" shouted Louise.

She promptly called her mother back East.

"Steven Spielberg is doing his first animated series ever, *Tiny Toons*, and he's designed a character that fits me to a *T*," she bubbled, wondering if Spielberg even knew she existed.

No matter how right the casting director thought she was for the part, this was Hollywood, and performers had to prove themselves by auditioning. Louise prayed all the way to the studio that she'd make the famous director pleased by his insight in selecting her.

She arranged the pages of the script on the music stand in front of her, adjusted her headphones, and waited for the casting director's cue.

In her mind, she had warmed to this rabbit. She imagined a funny, dynamic cartoon star with great lines and series stature. She was already thinking how she could invent some signature one-liners for the character—utterances that everyone would remember, like Fred Flintstone's, "Yabbadabbadoo" . . . or Bugs Bunny's, "Eh, what's up, Doc?"

The casting director motioned for her to start.

When Louise opened her mouth, she was shocked. A

cracked croak emerged. The more she tried to speak, the more hoarse she became.

"Oh, no," she rasped. "I can't believe this!"

The casting director came into the studio, handed her tea, and quietly suggested she relax. Louise felt an arm on her shoulder, with comforting words: "Don't worry. We've got a week to make our recommendations. Come back then. We'll get it."

All the way home, Louise could not fathom why she'd had no warning that something was wrong with her voice. This was a totally new experience. She'd never lost her voice in several years of doing voice work.

She stopped at a drugstore and bought every throat remedy she could find, seeking speedy recovery.

Over the next week, she only had bad news to report to the casting director, who anxiously monitored Louise's progress on a daily basis. The deadline was extended, but Louise's voice failed to improve.

Eventually she heard the words she dreaded: "I'm sorry, Louise. We've got to move on."

What devastation! She was heartbroken.

For weeks she wondered, *Why? Why did this happen, God? That was my part!*

Then she did the only thing she could do—she got on with life.

WHEN GOD WINKS AT YOU

She did, after all, have an active career. In fact, one of two *Showtime* specials was about to be telecast, and when she was back in full voice, her producers asked her to go to New York City for a promotional appearance on *Good Morning America*.

It was during that trip that Louise experienced another unbelievable godwink. On a whim, she took in a hot Broadway show, *Catskills on Broadway*.

"An odd feeling came over me as I entered the Lunt Fontaine Theater," she recalled. "A feeling that I belonged there."

After the show, she and her friend decided to do the "in" thing—grab a bite at Sardi's famous theatrical restaurant.

They talked about the fun and simplicity of a show that starred three famous comedians—Freddie Roman, Dick Capri, and Mal Z. Lawrence, each with a history of performance in Catskill Mountain resorts—and the lone woman, impressionistic singer Marilyn Michaels.

Louise was just starting to tell her companion about the strange feelings she had upon entering the theater when a waiter brought drinks to the table.

"Compliments of the gentlemen behind you," said the waiter, nodding to the benefactors.

Rising from his chair, wearing a large grin, was Freddie Roman—from the show they had just seen.

"Louise, you won't believe this! I was just telling the guys,

'If Marilyn Michaels ever leaves the show, I know just the person who could do it. Louise DuArt . . . I met her on a Vegas talk show one time, but I don't know how to reach her.' What a coincidence. I look up and there you are!"

The next few weeks were a whirlwind. It turned out that Marilyn Michaels *was* leaving the show, and Louise was asked to fill in for two weeks. She won the hearts of audiences, and at the end of the trial run, she won the part.

> Things turn out best for the people who make the best of the way things turn out.[4]
>
> —JOHN WOODEN, COACH

"It was a dream bigger than I could possibly believe," she recollected. "A starring role on Broadway had been placed right in my lap through an unbelievable godwink."

Only on reflection did everything start to make sense. She realized that if she had won the part that was "perfect for her"—Spielberg's impressionist rabbit in *Tiny Toons*—she wouldn't have been available to take on something even bigger—a starring role on Broadway.

Through the clarity of hindsight, she now sees God's tapestry. The Broadway show changed her life—paving the path for the happiness she has today. This, she quietly acknowledges in conversation with God, was clear evidence of the power of unanswered prayer.

:: :: ::

THE HIDDEN BLESSING

The next time one of those earth-shattering things happens to you—a rotten medical report like Giuliani's, a disaster like Ruth Fertel's, or an opportunity lost like Louise's—take a moment to reflect on unanswered prayers. It is God's way of moving you from one direction to another.

At the time it will be painful. It will shock and assault your psyche. You'll want to throw a rock through a window or bang your head on a wall.

But you won't.

Instead, I hope you will lift this book off the shelf and reread this chapter, comparing your situation with the ones I've told you about.

Then get yourself that Garth Brooks CD and play it as loud as you can stand. Sing along about how God's unanswered prayers are among His greatest gifts.

CHAPTER SEVEN

GOD WINKS JUST IN TIME

Invariably, people send stories to me about moments when a wink from God auspiciously entered into their lives—just in time—delivering them from disaster or misfortune.

Or delivering them *good* news—just in time.

"God is never late—but He often arrives in the nick of time," is something my grandmother, Mama Alice, always said in that British accent of hers.

I suspect that we've all heard that adage, and probably endorse it more and more the older and wiser we get. In fact, most of the stories in this book could have fallen into this chapter, exemplifying that God's winks, *most* of the time, come *just* in time.

Here are a few of my favorite stories that support Mama Alice's premise.

GOD CALLING

The kitchen floor was littered with ripped-open cereal boxes, a dirty shirt, wadded newspaper, a spilled can of coffee—it was a mess.

In the middle of it all, sprawled Ron Latoure, sobbing uncontrollably.

His life was a mess.

Unbathed for days, matted hair swinging annoyingly in front of his eyes, Ron struggled to release an ice cube from a frozen tray.

"Damn you!" he cried, banging it on the floor.

Since his girlfriend, Donna, suddenly left him—the stinging words, "I'm fed up with you, your job, and everything about you!" ringing in his ears—he seemed to be drawn into a downward, spiraling whirlpool. The breakup was all his fault. And now he was certain he really loved her—and should have told her so.

"Damn youuuu."

His self-esteem had never been lower. He was worthless. He was of no use to anyone. And nobody cared.

Snap.

An ice cube broke from the pack. He watched his skin redden as he roughly scraped the cold cube across his wrist. It would deaden the pain.

The knife would deaden him.

"Auuuugggggg!" A guttural, desperate, primeval sound erupted from his depths as he lifted the knife.

"He was the sweetest guy you'd ever want to meet," said producer Bryan Hickox to his wife Joanne, describing the events that had taken place on the set of a production he'd just completed.

"Ron Latoure is one of the best DPs in the business," he continued, recounting the erratic behavior of his director of photography. "But I'm worried about him."

He described how he'd had to pull Ron aside to talk with him about his uncharacteristic tardiness and outbursts during the filming. Quietly pausing, Bryan pictured his last conversation with him:

"Ron, you're a mess," he'd said in a fatherly manner.

Ron hung his head, nodding in agreement.

"I've got a friend you should talk to. Larry Poland. He might help you out."

Dr. Larry Poland, founder of Mastermedia Ministries, was a friend and counselor to many who work in the television and film industry.

Joanne interrupted his thoughts with an observation:

"Sounds like he really got hit hard when Donna walked out on him," she said thoughtfully.

Bryan nodded. "She had a hard time handling Ron's busy travel schedule." Sadly shaking his head, he added, "He's really depressed."

"Why don't we invite him to dinner?" offered Joanne softly.

Bryan looked at her.

It was a highly uncharacteristic remark. Joanne did not normally invite someone from one of Bryan's productions to their home. Certainly she was a gracious hostess. They would often dine out with colleagues or even have an occasional dinner party.

But . . . inviting one of the staff to dinner . . . that was different.

"Good idea," said Bryan, going to the phone.

There was no answer.

Joanne continued to think about Ron. Something was really pressing on her mind that they should reach out to him.

"I'm going to try him again," she said after a while.

"Quieeeeett!" screamed Ron, once more swiping the ice over his wrist.

Through the maelstrom of internal and external screams broke an aggravating noise.

Ringggggg.

Ringggggg.

"Quieeeeett!"

The blade wavered above his wrist. He paused.

"H-h-hello?"

"Hi, Ron. This is Joanne Hickox. Bryan and I were hoping you could join us for dinner tonight at our house.

"Ah . . ." He was at a loss for words.

"Can you make it?"

"Ah . . . yeah . . . I guess so."

Bryan greeted Ron at the door, and before sitting down to dinner, he gave his director of photography a little tour of their home, commenting upon the relevance of particular artwork and giving brief descriptions of how he had acquired them.

In the hallway hung an oil painting by an artist that Bryan knew personally. It was an unusual depiction of Jesus. Smiling.

Ron stared at the painting.

He felt strange. These nice people inviting him into their home—making him feel important, appreciated. And now, looking at the image of Christ smiling—at *him!* He felt a sudden constriction in his throat. Tears welled up. He couldn't help it. He wept.

Placing an arm on Ron's shoulder, Bryan sensed he was

witnessing the start of a transformation. One that needed Larry Poland's help to complete.

Two days later, over breakfast with Larry at a Denny's restaurant, Ron committed his life to the Lord.

Only later did Bryan Hickox learn that Joanne's telephone call was a godwink—just in time.

"What are the odds that you would call Ron at that exact moment?" Bryan pondered aloud to Joanne. "Wasn't it incredible how God nudged you into inviting him to dinner?"

Ron Latoure looks back on that evening with thankfulness. He stood on the precipice of his own demise, convinced that no one cared about him. But the unbelievable timing of the call from Joanne Hickox—God winking at him just in time to save his life—opened his consciousness to understanding that he was *never* alone, that Jesus was always smiling upon him.

> Here is a test to find whether your mission on Earth is finished: If you are alive, it isn't.[1]
> —RICHARD BACH

Since that day, Ron uses that extraordinary experience—the lifesaving godwink story—to witness to others. He tells how God winked at him, just in time, just in the moment he most needed it.

THE CLOWNS WEREN'T HOME

It may seem odd, but when a circus performer talks about "home," they are speaking about their apartment on the circus train where they live most of the year.

The annual schedule is pretty much the same. Exhaustive rehearsals at winter quarters, followed by opening night in St. Petersburg, Florida, in late December, building to the opening in New York City in March. Then it's on the rails for the rest of the season.

This is the story of the decisions made by four residents of the community we know as the Ringling Bros. and Barnum & Bailey Circus:

- Tammy and Tommy Parish, the famous clown couple whose colorfully painted faces were smiling from billboards and the sides of buses in every major city;
- Jim Ragona, a handsome ringmaster entering his thirteenth season, who as a child had prophetically announced in his fantasy play the words, "Ladies and gentlemen, welcome to the 'The Greatest Show on Earth'"; and
- David Kiser, a gregarious natural organizer who was also commencing his thirteenth year of clowning.

Each of these performers should have been at home on the evening of January 12, 1994. Because they weren't, their lives were saved. Extraordinary godwinks intervened, just in time.

Two weeks earlier, on the opening night of the circus, Tammy and Tommy Parish became the parents of a new baby clown named Amelia. (Whimsically, I've wondered if Amelia entered the world with bright red dots on her cheeks.)

Tammy Parish was exhausted. Amelia was born by cesarean section, and though Tammy had not yet returned to center ring, she was hard at work behind the scenes. On the night of January 12, she longingly anticipated crawling into her bed and having a day off as the circus train was about to move on to Orlando.

Tommy had decided to drive the family car to Orlando rather than have it sent. He urged Tammy to come with him.

"Come on, you and Amelia can sleep in the car! We'll get a hotel and have the day to play."

"Tommy, you know I always sleep better at home. Besides, the baby is still a light sleeper."

"Come on, honey! I just want my girls to be with me."

She relented.

As a normal rule, Jim Ragona also arranged to have his car sent ahead as the circus moved from city to city. That allowed him to sleep in his apartment on the train, which he'd newly decorated, and still have transportation when he arrived at his destination.

But on January 12, Jim wrestled with whether he should drive to Orlando. He had not booked a place to stay. And he, too, needed a good night's rest.

"In the end, because it was a relatively short hop, I decided to drive—to have a real day off in Orlando," he said.

David Kiser had no question about what he was doing on January 12. Well in advance, he had spread the word to the other clowns that he was organizing a day of pure fun at Walt Disney World. In a scene mimicking the circus itself, he piled ten clowns and himself into a five-passenger minivan to make the two-hour drive to Orlando. Two additional clowns arranged to meet the group there. None of the thirteen clowns would be at home that night.

The circus train pulled out of St. Petersburg in the early morning of January 13. Shortly before 9:00 AM, a man stopped at a railroad crossing near Lakeland and watched as the colorful train passed. He noticed sparks flying from beneath one of the cars and instantly called 911 on his cell phone.

The sparks were caused by a broken wheel directly under the clown car. At forty miles an hour the train rapidly approached a junction. All the cars on the front of the train glided over the junction, but when the broken wheel encountered the switch, the remaining thirteen cars, from the clown car to the caboose, violently careened from the track in a screech of ripped metal, cantilevering in every direction, landing like broken toys.

The train was strewn along the tracks, spilling into the backyard of a Lakeland home, which within minutes became an emergency medical center for the injured. Only later did people ponder the irony that the home was owned by the father-in-law of a Ringling Brothers executive vice president, adding to a chain of godwinks.

Tammy and Tommy Parish and Jim Ragona rushed to the scene. They learned that elephant trainer Ted Sverteski and performer Cesilee Conkling had lost their lives in the tragedy.

As they surveyed the devastation, they could only marvel at the godwinks that had caused so many to be saved.

"It's mind-boggling that so many people were away from home that night, and there were not more injuries," said Tammy. "Our bedroom was demolished. Where the baby would have been . . . was crushed."

"At first, I couldn't find my home," said Jim Ragona. "Then I realized that the two outside walls of the train were pressed together, actually touching each other. My bed . . . where I would have been sleeping . . . was crushed between them."

David Kiser also let out a sigh, observing that his bedroom was directly above the broken wheel.

Moreover, because most of the people on the train were still in bed at the time of the crash, injuries were minimized.

Told that it was the worst circus disaster ever, the circus family did what families must do at times of crisis: they came before the Lord, pulled themselves together, mourned the loss of two of their own, and honored God for the blessing that so many were saved.

When they opened in Orlando, delayed by only one night, the circus family was lifted up by the warm embrace of a supportive and exuberant audience.

In subsequent years, Tammy, Tommy, Jim, and David have wondered if God underscored His presence in their lives by using the number 13: on January 13, as David and Jim entered their 13th year with the circus, and as 13 clowns took a trip to Walt Disney World, 13 cars tore from the track.

This is for certain: they'll never let a January 13 pass without a special prayer of thanks to God for placing them where they were, just in time.

WHEW!

The day was slipping away.

Mary Jane Waldorf fleetingly looked at the clock, anxiously

hoping she'd conquer this new chicken recipe before her husband got home. Cooking was not her forte.

Maybe I shouldn'ta taken this on tonight, she thought.

With a motherly glance, she saw that Kurt, her four-year-old, was still busy playing with a coloring book and crayons in the middle of the kitchen floor.

She smiled, watching the intent look on his face as the crayon moved across the page and outside the lines.

Her attention was drawn back to the chicken. Why was this so hard? Aren't women supposed to be born knowing how to cook a simple meal? But this recipe was asking for things she didn't understand.

A sudden, irrational idea flashed into her mind. A momentary escape from this frustration.

"Come on, Kurt . . . let's you and me hang that teddy bear picture I bought for your room."

Scooping up her son, Mary Jane knew that *this* was a task she could handle with ease. *That chicken can just wait,* she thought.

After placing a hook in the bedroom wall, she stepped back, tilted her head slightly, and said, "How's that?" looking at her son.

Crash!

It was the sound of breaking glass coming from elsewhere in the house.

Mary Jane ran to the kitchen and was flabbergasted. The chandelier had fallen from the ceiling and smashed to smithereens—right where Kurt had been sitting only moments before!

Looking at the shards of glass and splintered metal, Mary Jane breathed a sigh of relief and rolled her eyes skyward, acknowledging the wonderful godwink that had "unreasonably" motivated her to leave her cooking chores, to scoop up Kurt, and to take him to safety—just in the nick of time.

Isn't It Amazing?

If you totaled up the number of times you were just about to step off a curb but were distracted by something, when you found yourself almost striding in front of a fast-moving car, when a small voice deep within—just in the nick of time—stopped you from taking that step, I suspect you'd be amazed. Sometimes called *instinct*, I call it *the small, still voice of God*.

MORNING SOUNDS

"Readyyyy . . ."

The captain's gruff voice echoed through the barren barracks.

Slap!

In near unison, fourteen hands slapped cold muzzles, orchestrating the elevation of fourteen rifles into the frigid, post-dawn air.

Arnold Hutschnecker stared back at them.

How had he found himself in this predicament?

The words, *God, how are you going to get me out?* raced through his mind as he counted fourteen intent soldiers, in stone-statue postures, squinting back at him through crosshairs.

He was only twenty. A young soldier cut off from his German army unit, behind enemy lines in the Ukraine. He had banded together with six others, all older than him, but his headstrong personality had soon cast him as the leader. They'd found the deserted barracks for refuge, only to be awakened suddenly by Russian soldiers, rousted outside at the end of rifles, and shoved into a line two feet apart.

Pulling a deep breath to calm himself, Arnold surveyed his adversaries. Seven of the soldiers had fallen to one knee, the other seven were standing. He quickly calculated: *Two rifles aimed at each victim. No escape. No place to run.*

Arnold thought of his family in Berlin.

He thought of God.

"Aaaaaim . . ."

The captain's voice, raspy from years of tobacco use, pierced the air like the cracking sound of a frozen lake. He paused. He took several long, savoring drags on the remainder of his hand-rolled cigarette.

A morning breeze whistled through the sparse trees and amongst the buildings.

The captain tossed the cigarette to the ground. He stomped on it, as if he were killing a bug, slowly twisting his boot to be certain of its death.

Above the breeze rose a faint sound. A purring sound.

The captain raised an eyebrow, cocked his head.

The noise increased. Soon it was identifiable as a motorbike, coming closer and closer. The bike and its rider sped into the yard. A hurried statement in a foreign language caused the captain to shout a command.

Arnold didn't comprehend the words, but he knew they meant "Move out!" as the firing squad scattered.

Arnold motioned for his soldiers to shrink back behind the buildings.

"What's going on?" they asked.

"Polish Legionnaires . . . they must be coming this way! But run. They're our enemies too!"

As World War I wound down, Arnold Hutschnecker led his compatriots to safety and made his way home to Berlin. Only a few years later, his Jewish heritage was exposed, and he fled to America from the country he'd defended. His postwar studies allowed him to become a prominent doctor in medicine and psychology, and in the mid-1950s, he wrote a best-selling book aptly titled *The Will to Live*.

Arnold's book drew upon the wisdom he'd gained about the power of faith as he stood—with seemingly no escape—before a firing squad on a frigid morning in the Ukraine.

> You cannot do a kindness too soon, for you never know how soon it will be too late.[2]
>
> —RALPH WALDO EMERSON

When a close friend found himself with the rare opportunity to coax Arnold into a personal reflection on those distant events, the doctor confessed that he'd often marveled at the godwinks that had so auspiciously arrived—just in time—to cause the captain to drag slowly on the remnants of his cigarette, producing an opportunity for a distant motorbike to be heard, and to lift Arnold from a seemingly hopeless situation.

SING A SONG OF BLUE

The wild, squeal-filled game of tag ended when Dave and his two little sons collapsed on the grass, blinking up at an ice-blue sky. It was the first time he had seen Dagyn and Devin in seven days. He had picked them up at their mom's for a weekend of roughhousing and snuggling.

As they lay on their backs, breathing hard and blinking up into the brilliant sun, five-year-old Dagyn spoke. "Why is the sky blue, Dadda?" he asked in the confiding way of children, never doubting that mommy and daddy have all the answers they need.

Dave smiled, amazed at the happy coincidence behind this question. Three days ago it would have stumped him. But studying for a teaching degree, Dave was taking a physics class this term. Just two days before, his professor had discussed the science behind the simple phenomenon.

In his best teacher's voice, Dave began: "Light comes from the sun, right Dagyn?"

"Right, Dadda!"

"And did you know that the air has tiny, invisible things in it called molecules? We can't see the molecules, but sometimes a bunch of them clump together, and we get rain. Water is one kind of molecule, but there are others too; we just can't see them. Are you with me so far?"

"Yes, Dadda!"

"Well, the light from the sun has lots of different colors in it. You know that prism Mommy has, the glass thing that when you put it in the sun, all the colors of the rainbow shine out? Those colors are all the colors hiding in sunlight. Well, blue is one of those colors, and when the blue light bumps into the tiny molecules in the air, the molecules grab that blue color and bounce it around the sky. They like blue the best, the molecules do, and when they scatter the blue light around—like pixies scattering fairy dust—you see a blue sky."

"Wow," Dagyn answered softly, shifting his head on Dave's chest so he could feel the vibrations of his father's voice. It was one of his favorite snuggle positions.

Dave smiled. It was a happy moment.

That moment was a rare idyll in a sea of turbulence. He was sure he had contributed to the marital turmoil that caused his wife to leave him two years before, but he couldn't help feeling depressed and resentful. She'd moved in with a man who abused the boys physically and verbally. When Dave went to the authorities, the boys clammed up, afraid that if they told they would have to go live in a foster home.

He felt abandoned by the system that was meant to protect his kids. And by God—if God even existed.

Days later, alone again late at night in a deserted dental office, Dave wiped down counters, vacuumed carpets, and washed the windows that reflected back his own haggard face. He had attended classes all day and had just begun his swing-shift job as a janitor. The problem with a lonely, mind-less job like this was that it was too easy to add up your troubles.

Depressed, Dave didn't turn on the office radio to keep him company as he usually did. The radio sat high on a shelf in the patient records alcove, and tonight he just didn't have the energy to reach up and switch it on. He walked straight into one of the examination rooms and began cleaning the floor in silence, his anguished thoughts filling his head to the bursting point.

He wasn't worth anything, to anyone. His ability to stick with school was doubtful. After all, he'd dropped out many times before. He could hear his own dad telling him he was useless. When Dave tried to follow his directions, his dad sneered, "Do I have to draw you a picture? Are you stupid?"

Now, he couldn't even protect his own children. Each time he complained to Children's Services, his kids suffered more because of his speaking out. What kind of parent was he, to let his children suffer? As he wiped off a counter, he picked up the photo one of the hygienists kept of her kids: two blond, blue-eyed cuties. His eyes filled as he thought of Dagyn's trusting face, that same face clouded with confusion when he asked Dave why his mom's boyfriend liked to hit him.

He was a failure as a father, just as his own dad had failed him.

He replayed the words he heard his father say every time he got angry: "I'm going to kill myself!"

Tears brimmed in his eyes.

It was time.

Dave mentally turned to a familiar scenario—his "final solution." On the ten-mile drive home from his job, he pictured how it would end. A part of the highway was lined with hundred-year-old valley oaks. He would get up speed on the straightaway just before the trees, jerk the wheel to the right, and within seconds there'd be nothing left but a tangled clump of steel and a broken, lifeless body. His old Bonneville, from pre-airbag days, would become his coffin.

He pictured what an oak tree would look like from behind the windshield of his car as the tree emerged out of the fog, growing larger in his headlights—then, total peaceful blackness. No noise, no sadness, no fear, nothing.

He resolved to do it. Tonight would be the night.

Strangely calm, almost elated that he'd made a clear decision, Dave lowered the blinds and left the examination room, shutting the door behind him.

For the last time, he thought, dragging his cart into the alcove.

He stopped. He heard music.

Funny, he hadn't heard it before. The radio was piped into all the rooms that he'd been cleaning for the last thirty minutes. He knew he hadn't turned it on.

"Who's there?" Dave shouted, thinking someone must have come in. But no, the security door would have buzzed.

That's weird, he thought, shrugging it off, lifting his mop out of the pail.

Then he froze, mop suspended in midair. He couldn't shrug off what his ears were hearing now. Something like: "Daddy, why's the sky so blue? When I grow up, will I be just like you?"[3]

As the song continued, Dave stared dumbly at the speaker in the ceiling and collapsed to his knees. Like a first-class letter, someone had just addressed a message to him. He'd never heard this song before, and there it was—a message bouncing out over the airwaves.

For him. A radio turned on by an unseen power.

For him. He was sure of that.

A flood of tears washed over him, and he was engulfed in the most incredible feeling of love and release of pain. A feeling like he'd never known before.

But the warm embrace of love was followed by a jolt of sheer terror.

What am I doing? If I kill myself, there will be no one there to protect Dagyn and his little brother.

Within seconds his "final solution" was revealed as a ridiculous idea. What someone once called *a permanent solution to a temporary problem.*

"I knew then, there was a God," said Dave later. "I knew He loved me, and that He was there to protect me and teach me, just like I'm here to protect and teach my kids.

"That night was a wake-up call, a turning point in my life. I still have problems with depression. My boys continued to have problems with their mom's boyfriend until the courts finally granted a restraining order against him. But if that radio hadn't come on when it did, I would not be here today. That godwink gave me the courage and conviction to carry on. It was the ultimate 'hang in there.'

"There is a God. And you can connect with Him if you will only try," said Dave.

Dave learned the song he heard was "Father's Love," by Bob Carlisle and Randy Thomas:

"Daddy, why's the sky so blue today?
Does Jesus really hear me when I pray?"[4]

THE GIVER OF A GIFT

Matt had a feeling that Cory was just one of those kids, the kind of high-school freshman that others picked on—glasses, shy, just a little too nice. That Friday afternoon Cory looked

< 158 >

somewhat lost, walking down the sidewalk ahead of Matt, with a huge armful of books.

Why would any classmate of mine be taking that many books home on a Friday? wondered Matt. *He must be a nerd.* After all, it was a football weekend with several parties going on.

Just then a bunch of boisterous boys dashed past Matt, catching up to Cory.

"Hey, watch out!" they shouted, sending the stack of books flying in every direction, accidentally-on-purpose. As Cory went tumbling, his glasses flew into the grass, and the scoundrels kept right on running—two of them turning to reveal large, self-satisfied grins.

Cory was searching the ground for his glasses when Matt approached him. He looked up, his eyes filled with sadness.

"Those guys are jerks," said Matt angrily, leaning down to pick up Cory's glasses and helping him gather his books.

"I'm Matt Smitt," he said with an outstretched hand.

Cory's face lit up with a sweet smile.

Offering to help carry some of his books, Matt learned as they walked along that Cory had recently transferred to their school and lived fairly close to him. Arriving at Cory's house, Matt again extended his hand.

"Hey, there's a party after the game tomorrow, you wanna come?"

Cory looked surprised.

"Yeah. That would be great," he replied.

As the school year wore on, the more Matt got to know Cory, the more he liked him. And over the course of the next three years, the two became close friends. Cory began to model Matt's confident, good-natured personality. He opened up, was less shy, and more and more people wanted to be his friend.

Cory, in turn, was a good support for Matt and others. He was better at math and science and had better study habits than most kids. Cory began helping those who were struggling. Because he was better grounded than many, they looked to him as a moral compass.

Matt and Cory hung out together, double-dated, and shared dreams for the future.

But there was something that Cory never shared with Matt. Not until graduation.

Cory had been named class valedictorian. He was nervous, knowing he had to make a speech.

"Hey, you're gonna be great!" said Matt with a pat on the shoulder, as they stood in their hats and gowns.

Cory smiled and nodded "thanks."

A few minutes later Cory stood before his classmates and faculty and spoke with an authoritative yet slightly tremulous voice.

"Graduation is a time to thank those who helped you make

it through those tough years," he said, "your parents, your teachers, your siblings, maybe a coach . . . but mostly, your friends. I am here to tell you that being a friend to someone is the best gift you can give them. I am going to tell you a story—"

Cory took himself back to that day when he was new at school. He was the geeky kid with glasses. No one liked him. He was out of place. And he had decided to end it all over a weekend—to take his own life. Who'd care?

He did have considerate thoughts for his mom . . . how tough it would be for her to carry home all the books he'd collected in his locker after he was gone. So he decided to empty his locker on that Friday afternoon.

Then he told how a gang of kids came along and sent him sprawling to the ground with all his things flying everywhere, including his glasses.

Cory looked into the audience, directly at Matt, and smiled.

"Thankfully, I was saved that day," he said, slowing his cadence. "I was saved from doing the unspeakable by someone who leaned down to help me up, who cheered me up and cheered me on . . . not just that day . . . but every day since. I would like to thank him now. My friend—Matt Smitt."

Matt sat stunned.

Who knew what Cory had been planning on that Friday nearly four years earlier? Who knew what a godwink it was for him to have been there just in time, and done what was in his heart to do?

Cory ended with a poem.

> When someone's lost, aimless, and adrift,
> Take the time, give 'em a lift.
> Yesterday is history, tomorrow is a mystery,
> But today, *you* can be their gift.

:: :: ::

IF YOU THINK ABOUT IT . . .

Yes, if you really took the time to think about it, you probably have a story of your own that could have gone into this chapter. Maybe several. Events that have long since slipped into the recesses of your mind, which you once granted the attention of a mere moment before shrugging them off as good fortune.

It is useful to resurrect those stories once in a while, reminding yourself that God has nudged you, spoken to you, or caused some other action to occur that pulled you back from the brink of calamity through a personally delivered godwink—just in time.

CHAPTER EIGHT

GOD WINKS ON FAMILY

I have long held the secret notion that when my tear ducts become involuntarily activated, it is substantiation that the Holy Spirit is moving through me. This is especially true with matters of family. Recalling one of my dad's familiar habits or coming across a sweet, child-made birthday card can prompt a wetting of my cheeks. I also find my tear drops are triggered at family gatherings or simply upon receipt of a handwritten note from my dear mother.

The love we have for family is tethered to our hearts by bloodlines and emotions quite distinct from nonfamily. These deep-seated bonds are also likely to activate abundant godwinks, reaffirming God's joy with our celebration of family.

WHEN GOD WINKS AT YOU

He is pleased by the love we show our spouses, parents, children, and brothers and sisters. And as we display kindness to kin, we can expect godwinks for us, exemplified by the stories I have collected for this chapter.

FOSTERING FAITH

"Come on kids . . . let's get going! We want to get there before dark."

Laura Saldivar was ushering her three older children—eleven, thirteen, and fifteen—and her three younger foster children—eight months, one, and four—into the eight-seater SUV for a week's camping at Fairy Stone State Park near Martinsville, Virginia.

"Emerson, can you carry the baby's bag, please?"

She shouted the good-natured command to her oldest son while aiding the younger ones along and carrying one-year-old Dion, the foster baby whom she'd grown to love like her own since he was three days old.

"Come on . . . everybody's got a job."

Seasoned by her own service in the U.S. Navy—where she and Carlos had met, fallen madly in love, and married fifteen years earlier—Laura was commanding her own small army on their way to a long-talked-about summer vacation. Unfortunately, Carlos had to stay behind in Virginia Beach to work.

Laura and Carlos were ideal foster parents. Deeply committed to their faith, they had a heart for children who were victims of society's underbelly—children who came under the Child Protective Services division of the Virginia Department of Social Services. For seven years CPS social workers knew they could call on Laura and Carlos in the middle of the night, and they would always open their arms to children who needed to be sheltered.

"They knew they could call me, and I'd always say yes," said Laura, anticipating the next question. "Take care of 'em 24/7 . . . but don't bond too much . . . those are the orders."

For several weeks prior to the camping trip, however, she and Carlos had seriously been talking with the foster care social workers about adopting Dion—having found it impossible *not* to bond with this adorable child.

Arriving at Fairy Stone Park, Laura and the kids set up the pop-up trailer tent, pulled their bikes from the carrier on the SUV, and soon were singing songs and toasting marshmallows around the campfire. Laura's own children accepted their mother's counsel to always help the smaller ones. They also accepted that there would be times when the babies would get more of their mother's attention.

"They all understood that the foster children came from less-privileged backgrounds than themselves, and they sometimes needed more attention," she said.

At the end of the second day, one of the older children, a responsible teenager, asked if she could take Dion for a ride on the bike. The girl would hold Dion on the seat and walk him around as she had done in their own neighborhood.

"Just be careful," Laura intoned hesitantly.

But moments later, she wished she'd said no.

"Mommy, Mommy . . . the bike fell over . . . Dion's been hurt!" cried the girl, rushing to Laura with Dion screaming in her arms.

Laura's heart sank.

"Aw, Baby, you'll be all right," she said cuddling Dion, soothing his tears, thinking his ankle had twisted and would soon be better.

She thought she ought to have a doctor take a look at him, to be on the safe side, and was directed by a park ranger to a hospital in Martinsville, twenty miles away.

Doctors took X-rays and reported that Dion had suffered a twisted fracture, perhaps catching his foot in the spokes of the bike as he fell. He would need to stay overnight. Because hospital policy required that a child not be left alone overnight, Laura and the five other children bunked in the room.

Laura advised doctors that Dion was a foster child, which mandated that they report the matter to the local office of the Department of Social Services.

"When there's a twisted fracture to a foster child, that's a red flag," said Laura, fully understanding why the department was routinely called. But she was not prepared for what followed.

Within hours, social workers came to the hospital and took custody of the other two foster children and ordered Laura to remain overnight with Dion. The next day, he was also taken from her.

Laura cried daily for the next seventy days, saddened by the sudden absence of children she loved. She was shocked when the social workers, who for years had praised her foster parenting, now accused her of neglect. They refused to return phone calls and avoided conversations with her.

"People who knew me well were acting like they didn't know me—that I was a bad mother," she said. "Only one person stood up for me—but only in private beause she was fearful of losing her job."

Laura and Carlos determined that filing for adoption was their only option. Dion was the only one of their three foster children who was adoptable at that time, and they decided to instigate proceedings for custody against the wishes of the Department of Social Services.

Within weeks they were summoned to a hearing at juvenile court.

The judge patiently listened to the accusations of the DSS attorney against Laura. The charges of neglect were spelled out carefully and seemingly callously.

"I had to muster all my strength not to show anger," said Laura quietly, "but it was very, very hurtful to hear those words."

The judge then asked Laura's attorney to testify. He detailed her history of exemplary service—how she and her family had opened their home to some twenty-five homeless babies and children over seven years. He articulately described the innocence of the accident that injured Dion and suggested that a far more serious injury to the child's psyche would be the child's deprivation of this loving family.

The judge was unsatisfied. He set another hearing in thirty days to hear additional testimony from authorities in Martinsville who were involved on the night of the accident.

> Kindness is more important than wisdom. The recognition of this is the beginning of wisdom.[1]
>
> —THEODORE ISAAC RUBIN, MD

Laura was worried. The days ticked off slowly, each a burdensome uncertainty. She prayed, *Lord, please allow me to have my baby back.*

At the second hearing, the judge heard additional testimony from the DSS and the painful charges of parental neglect were repeated. They said that the injury to the child proved that Laura Saldivar was unfit to be a foster mother or to have custody of little Dion.

The judge looked directly at the social workers and their attorney.

"A few days ago my son suffered a broken bone when he fell from the trampoline in my backyard," said the judge pointedly. "Would you come and take him away from me?"

There was nervous laughter.

"Oh no, judge, he's your blood child," replied the attorney.

"So, you're telling me that this mother, whose record you have testified was exemplary for seven years, would not have had this child taken from her if she was the blood parent?"

They sullenly nodded. "Yes, sir."

"There are many times as a judge, when I go home at night wondering if I have made the right decision. Today I am confident that this baby belongs with his mother."

He slammed the gavel.

Laura was surprised later that evening as she stood in line

at Wal-Mart. Someone was calling her name, trying to get her attention.

She turned. She didn't recognize him at first. It was the judge from the hearing, no longer in a robe, but dressed in street clothes. He was smiling. Laura felt she could now communicate in a way she could not in the courtroom.

She went to him and hugged him.

Then she pointed to Dion in the shopping cart. "This is the baby you returned to me today."

She squeezed the judge again.

"I felt badly that his son was injured in the trampoline accident," said Laura later. "But I wonder how things would have turned out if that godwink hadn't happened."

FROM HEARTACHE TO HAPPINESS

The birth was easy, or as easy as it could be for an unmarried seventeen-year-old girl. The hard part was yet to come.

She sat up in her hospital bed, her face streaked with tears, looking hopefully at Danella Hoff.

"Nurse, I'd like to spend some time with my baby," said the young mother.

Danella frowned.

She knew the rules—it was not a good idea to let birth mothers bond with their babies when an adoptive family was waiting in the wings. They needed to avoid complicating an already heartbreaking transition.

"Please . . ."

Danella relented.

In the nursery at St. Margaret's Hospital in Montgomery, Alabama, she walked quietly to the only bassinet labeled "adoption" and picked up a tiny baby boy. Wrapped snugly in his nursery blankets, he slept blissfully unaware of his already turbulent life. She planted a kiss on his forehead.

After delivering the baby to his mother's trembling, out-stretched arms, Danella retreated to a corner of the room.

The girl leaned her head to her son's face, touching her lips to his forehead, nose, and mouth. Love for the child swelled up until it burst out again, and a mother's tears christened her baby.

"I'll love you forever. Please forgive me, but you'll be better off with a mommy and daddy who can give you everything . . . that I can't," she sobbed.

All the stresses of the last nine months—an unplanned pregnancy, her family's hasty move to Montgomery to avoid the prying eyes of neighbors, and the decision to give the baby up—all of it melted away as the beauty of this little life over-whelmed her.

She gave him a name to be placed on the birth certificate even though she knew that someone else would choose another name for her child.

Wiping away her own tears and watching, Danella drew closer. This was no ordinary girl—one who could be oblivious to her mistake and probably on course to make another one. This was a woman-to-be with an almost superhuman ability to put aside her own desires to do what she believed to be best for her child.

Perching on the side of the bed, Danella hugged the young mother as she crooned over her baby.

"Everything will be all right. You'll be fine; the baby will be happy," said Danella soothingly, with words of comfort that felt hollow as she spoke them.

Little did she know that the scene she had just witnessed was the beginning of a long, slow godwink.

Danella's shift ended, and she went home to her husband.

For twenty years as she raised her daughter, Amanda, Danella helped bring hundreds of babies into the world, but she never forgot the purity of the love she saw that November night in 1980. She felt that she had received a gift that night, being witness to the purest love of all, *agape*—a love untainted by self-interest or desire. That love became a part of her work, part of her marriage, and part of how she parented her own child.

"Mom, this is the one!" Amanda exclaimed joyfully as she told Danella about the new man in her life, retelling how she and Chad had met and fallen in love over a long conversation at a coffee house. Amanda had just graduated from college and for the first time realized she had met a man who felt like he could be her lifetime partner.

"Well, when do I get to meet him?" Danella asked.

"Tomorrow!" Amanda said, the word lifting off her tongue like a dove in flight.

When Chad Brooks walked through the door the next day, Danella's maternal antennae went up. Chad exuded anger and a sense of longing though he smiled and exchanged pleasantries.

"What's your story, Chad?" Danella asked bluntly as they settled into the living room chairs for a get-to-know-you chat.

"Well, I've just finished an apprenticeship with a master electrician. I tried roofing, but that was too dull. I like the challenge of wiring an entire building. I'm pretty sure this is the field for me."

"What about your family?"

"My mom's name is Dot Clare. She and my dad divorced when I was a baby, and she married my stepdad when I was two."

"And are you from here?"

"Yes, I was born here, but my real parents aren't from here.

I mean, my mom isn't my birth mom; I was adopted. All I know is that my birth mom was from Colorado. She gave me away the night I was born."

The bitterness in Chad's voice cut like vinegar through the pleasant conversation.

Danella's hackles rose.

"Now wait a minute . . . let me tell you a story. I want you to know how much sacrifice and love goes into giving a baby up for adoption—a love that usually goes unrecognized. I've been lucky enough to witness it."

She retold the story of a night twenty-one years before, when she saw the greatest love of a mother for the baby she was giving up. Though she could barely recall the young girl's face, as Danella looked at Chad, a feeling rushed through her like a bolt of pure insight directly from the heavens above.

Could this be him? The very baby she was talking about . . . who was christened by his mother's tears that night in 1980?

She stopped midsentence and peered intently at Chad.

"How old are you?"

"Twenty-one."

Of course you are, she thought, as she studied Chad like a jeweler examining a precious gem. With growing wonder in her voice she asked: "Where were you born? Which hospital?"

"Jackson Hospital."

"Are you sure?" She realized this was a presumptuous question, but she sensed he was wrong.

"Yes, I'm sure . . . that's where my real mom gave me away."

Across the table, Amanda lifted an eyebrow, signaling her mother to let it go.

Danella dropped the subject.

Chad, unaware of the tension, didn't realize that his life was about to come full circle.

There were plenty of other topics to discuss as Amanda and Chad soon commenced plans for their wedding, which took place in December 2001.

During the early months of their marriage, from time to time, Danella urged Chad to request his adoption records, so he could find his birth mom and perhaps answer some of the questions that had nagged him all his life, causing deep bitterness.

But life was busy with work and family, and years passed.

Amanda became pregnant in March 2004. Feeling an urgency about his unborn baby's heritage, Chad finally requested from the state the file containing his birth records— a privilege offered adopted children when they turned twenty-one. As he sat reading the records at the kitchen table with Amanda and his mother-in-law, his eyes fell upon the birth date that matched his own. His birth mother was named Darla Svenby, and he was born at St. Margaret's Hospital in

Montgomery—where he knew Danella had worked—not Jackson Hospital.

Chad lifted his eyes and stared at his mother-in-law.

Danella knew what he'd read. She'd known it all along, from the day Amanda brought Chad home.

She nodded wordlessly as Chad's eyes widened.

"I have held you," Danella said tenderly. "And your mother loved you with the most unselfish love. Nobody loved you more than she did. Now go and find her."

Chad's godwink—the one that began the night he was born—had finally found its mark. With a sense of purpose he'd never felt before, he changed his last name to Svenby.

His and Amanda's search began in earnest with a flurry of "googling"—searching the Internet. Amanda typed in "Randy Allgood," the name of his birth father, and it brought up innumerable matches. They called them all; none panned out. "Darla Svenby" brought up absolutely no hits. But when in desperation Amanda combined the names, there was a hit! It led them to a list of addresses for the two. They were married!

"They're together!" Chad said in wonder. "If I find my mom, that means I've found my dad!"

A few days later Amanda's father, who had also been drawn into the search, handed them a folded piece of paper.

"Open it up, Chad," said Amanda.

His hands shaking, Chad unfolded the paper and read "Senior Master Sergeant Randy Allgood" with a telephone number for his work, at an Air Force base in Anchorage, Alaska.

He held the paper reverently and in a voice filled with awe, he said: "This is my dad, and this is his number!"

As he dialed the number, Chad didn't know what to say. He had thought of this conversation for years, and when it finally happened, all he could blurt out was: "Guess who this is!"

"Who is this?" was the brisk, military reply.

"I'm your son!" He had to repeat it a few times before Randy understood the meaning behind those simple words. The confusion lasted just a moment, and within minutes, floodgates burst open. For the next few weeks, the lines between Alabama and Alaska—cell phones, landlines, and e-mails—burned bright as Chad and his parents covered twenty-four years worth of love, longing, and heartache.

Chad absorbed his family history with amazement.

Two years following the chaotic early years of their relationship, Randy and Darla had married and parented four boys.

"Four brothers . . . I got more than I imagined!" marveled Chad, going instantly from an only child to an older brother.

Then another godwink unfolded: The name Darla put

down at the hospital for the baby she gave up was "Chad Svenby." His adoptive mother, totally unaware of that, had *also* named him Chad—Chad Brooks!

During their long-distance communication, Amanda and Chad put together another piece of their godwink puzzle. They learned that Chad's grandmother—Darla's mom—had prayed for Chad all her life. She faithfully wrote her never-seen grandson many letters over the years, trusting that some-day he would make his way back to his mother. When they heard that she died on March 2, 2004, the exact date the obstetrician had told Amanda that her and Chad's baby was conceived, they just shook their heads in disbelief.

> Before I formed you in the womb I knew you.
>
> —JEREMIAH 1:5 NKJV

Finally, it was time for Chad to close the circle. He longed to be held in the arms that had once enveloped him years before. He and Amanda flew to Alaska in the fall of 2004.

Just as she had twenty-four years earlier, Darla held out her arms to her baby as he emerged from the airport Jetway. For several moments, they clung to each other—heartache and sadness released in a torrent of tears.

"He clutched me so tightly, just like a little baby laying his head on my shoulder," she said as she spoke of their first meeting.

"Why, he's beautiful!" exclaimed Darla, sounding like a proud new mama as she pulled back to look at Chad.

Once he folded into his ready-made family, Chad wasn't about to leave. For three months, Amanda and he stayed with his parents and brothers—visiting, fishing, eating, laughing, learning, and crying.

"It's like he was the missing link to our family," said Darla.

"It's like we haven't missed a step," agreed Chad's dad, Randy. The past was no longer an unbearable, bitter, unresolved memory, but a welcome prelude to a future of close family ties.

Darla remembered: "That night in the hospital, I could hardly take it. I just didn't want to let go."

Now she doesn't have to, thanks to a steady stream of godwinks.

Twenty-one years in the making, the Godwink Link was an angel named Danella, who simply kept a memory alive for two decades and sensed her cue when it was time for her to do her part to bring a family back together again. Never could anyone have imagined that the baby Danella handed to a weeping mother would end up being her future son-in-law.

UNLUCKY DAY NO MORE

It was a hot Friday the thirteenth in July 1984, in Big Flat, Arkansas.

Angilee Wallis's phone rang.

Her twenty-year-old son Terry had been in an accident—a bad one. His truck had flipped, tumbled down a twenty-five-foot bank, and landed in a dry creek bed. He was rushed to a Missouri hospital—in a coma, near death.

After three months, Terry woke from his coma but couldn't speak. He was able to communicate only by blinking. He was out of critical condition, but no longer the smiling, proud dad that he had become when his daughter was born, just six weeks before the accident.

His eyes were open, and he was awake—but not aware.

He was not aware of how big his baby girl, Amber, was growing. Not aware as she grew into toddlerhood, entered grade school and then high school. He was not aware that Amber loved a daddy who could not love her back.

Several months after the tragedy, Terry was moved to a nursing home in Mountain View where he was visited by his wife, Sandra, as well as his brother, his parents, and, of course, Amber.

Years went by.

Every Friday the thirteenth, the family winced at the memory of that Friday in July, long ago. Not superstitious by nature, they still felt that bad luck had fallen on them that day.

Doctors reported that Terry's condition was not encouraging. His family—especially his mom—still kept visiting him, praying, and hoping.

After nineteen years, Angilee's prayers were finally answered. Terry woke up one morning like any other. Except for one thing—he greeted the day by speaking his first word in nearly two decades.

"Mom."

His family was shocked!

"I just fell over on the floor," said his mother, Angilee.

More words followed.

For a Father's Day present two days later, on June 15, Terry said, "Dad."

Although his speech was laborious, Terry slowly built up his vocabulary and long-term memory. And to the delight of his family, his sense of humor came back.

"It's amazing and uplifting," said Terry's doctor. "I think the message is that you should never give up hope."

"God gave us a miracle," said Angilee.

But just to let her know that it was Him—God—who was the author of this miracle, Terry awoke on another Friday the thirteenth . . . nineteen years after he had been silenced on that so-called unlucky day. God winked, and Terry Wallis started speaking again on Friday June 13, 2003.

THE NATURE OF FAMILY WINKS

I imagine that as you evaluate the godwinks in your life, like those in the preceding stories, they'll remind you of God's personal involvement in matters of family. Certainly each of the foregoing stories was a deeply heartfelt experience. But sometimes godwinks within the family tree are more serendipitous, as was the case with the next two stories.

A TALE OF TWO BARRYS

Joe and Percy Lyman were brothers—very close brothers. They enjoyed family holidays and vacations together. They went into business together, growing a small butcher shop into a robust supermarket in Harlem, a desirable area of Manhattan in those days. Their wives each gave birth to a daughter and

< 182 >

then a son. The boys—born one year apart—were both named Barry after a favored grandfather.

Barry Hugh and Barry Saul regularly played together, and they became best of friends—until Barry Hugh was ten. His father died suddenly in his forties. Within a short time, Barry Saul's father died too—they say of a broken heart.

Yet as close as the fathers were, the mothers were not. The families quickly drifted apart, ceasing all communications between the two Barrys.

Forty years passed.

Barry Hugh grew up to become a highly successful entrepreneur, the president of an electronics corporation. By his fiftieth year he had developed an expensive hobby—a keen interest in buying and selling antique British cars. Though he lived in Vermont, Barry had a friend named Tom who owned a classic car restoration company in New Jersey. He bought and sold several British cars in dealings with Tom and tried to visit the shop whenever he was in the area.

One day Barry walked into Tom's showroom specifically thinking about a vintage Morgan.

"Why are you thinking about a Morgan now?" asked Tom with a trace of annoyance. "You told me on the phone you were interested in the Austin Healy I advertised in the paper."

"I beg your pardon? I didn't call you," said Barry.

"I don't get it," continued Tom. "You phoned me about the ad. And every time I asked you a personal question, you said, 'I have no idea who you are.'"

As the penny began to drop, Barry slowly shook his head.

Could it be, he wondered, that his long lost cousin Barry Lyman had telephoned Tom? And that he was *also* a collector of classic cars made in Britain?

Barry laughed and gave Tom an explanation. Fortunately, the dealer still had the other Barry's number, and within moments the two Barrys were on the phone, emitting joyful sounds and arranging a luncheon appointment for the next day.

Talk about godwinks—both arrived at the restaurant driving the same model Mercedes. Both wore blue blazers, khakis, and a blue shirt. And both had an unusual watch on their wrists: a Concord Mariner SG.

It was a wonderful reunion, catching up on forty years lost. Barry Hugh learned that Barry Saul was also an entrepreneur, but in real estate management, and both men had arranged early retirement. Barry Hugh retired at fifty and Barry Saul would retire at fifty-three.

Nowadays the two Barrys live six houses apart in Delray Beach, Florida, and play golf a couple of times a week. Once again, they are the closest of friends.

BROTHERS WAFFLE

"I don't know why, I just feel like going to one of those waffle houses," said Rick Smith to his wife Marie. They were on the eighteen-hour, eleven-hundred-mile drive from visiting family in Pittsburgh to their home in Natchez, Mississippi.

"You don't like waffles," observed his wife.

"Yeah, well . . . I just have a hankering to try one of those waffle houses."

Marie cocked her head slightly and raised her eyebrows, tantamount to a shrug, thinking, *This too shall pass.*

A few minutes later, halfway along their drive somewhere outside of Nashville, she decided to test her husband's resolve.

"There's one!" she said, thinking he might say, "What?"—then she'd know the feeling had definitely passed.

"Naw, let's find another one," he replied.

They drove in silence for a while. Rick let his mind drift. He wondered how his brother Bob was doing—wished he could have seen him. A couple of weeks earlier, Bob had called to say he wouldn't be with them at the Pittsburgh family event because he would have to travel to San Antonio. In fact, he said his drive would take him right through Rick's town of Natchez.

"Well . . . why not stay at our house?" offered Rick. "I'll leave the keys for you."

"There's one." It was Marie, breaking into Rick's thoughts, pointing out a Waffle House.

"What's with this sudden waffle desire?" she continued, not waiting for a response. "There's another one. These people sure like waffles."

Rick was silent.

"So? That one looks okay. Come on, I'm getting hungry." Now she was really pressing the resolve button.

"Let's see what else there is," he murmured.

A half mile down the road, a fifth Waffle House emerged. They saw it simultaneously. Marie looked questioningly at Rick.

"Okay, let's stop at this one."

Inside, a line formed as a harried hostess said, "About a twenty-minute wait."

Marie rolled her eyes.

After five or ten minutes, Rick's impatience got the best of him.

"All right, let's go"—a statement equivalent to surrendering that once again he'd had a harebrained idea.

Sensing the potential loss of a customer, the hostess whispered: "There's a booth opening up right now, I'll get it cleaned up for ya."

Things were looking up. Soon the waffles arrived, and they tasted pretty darn good—much better than Rick had remembered.

As Rick looked for the waitress to request a check, his eyes landed on a lady who had just entered the restaurant.

"My gosh! That woman looks just like Beatrice," said Rick.

Marie turned. "And that man looks just like your brother Bob."

"It *is* Bob!"

Beatrice and Bob, and Rick and Marie squeezed into the booth. They marveled at the odds that would draw them together at this time and place—at this Waffle House, halfway between Pittsburgh and Natchez, actually, a bit out of the way on Bob and Beatrice's drive from San Antonio to Florida.

"How did you wind up coming this way?" asked Rick, still puzzled.

Bob shrugged, "We always wanted to see Nashville."

:: :: ::

TIES THAT BIND FAMILIES

I once heard a wise person say: "When love is close at hand, God's hand is close."

This collection of family stories underscores how godwinks seem to weave in and out of our lives more frequently among those with whom we have strong bonds of love.

As you interact with your family, look for these little coincidences and odd happenings, and see if you find this to be true.

CHAPTER NINE

GOD WINKS ON QUESTS

Nearly everyone has a quest.

Somewhere, you have always harbored a deep-seated notion of something you wanted to do. Maybe you have acted upon it, maybe you haven't. Perhaps you wished you were one of those persons who crossed the finish line at a twenty-six mile marathon—where winning wasn't the goal but just being in the race and finishing it.

Maybe you always wanted to write a book, perform on stage, or be the best golfer of anyone you know.

Perhaps you always wanted to do something to make a difference in other people's lives such as in a career or part-time volunteer service.

We are indoctrinated as children to begin thinking about our quests. People frequently ask, "What do you want to be when you grow up?"

I was in sixth grade when I toured a radio station, and my dream to be involved with radio and television was born.

My wonderful wife, Louise, knew from the time she watched *The Carol Burnett Show* on TV that when she grew up she wanted to be in show business (leading to multiple god-winks that eventually put her into a hit touring show with two of the stars of that show, Tim Conway and Harvey Korman).

Howard Jonas, the billionaire founder of IDT Communications, started a successful hot dog vending business as a kid.

Tiger Woods had a golf club in his hand almost as soon as he could walk.

Some people have a divine desire placed into their hearts at a very early age that becomes a beacon to follow like a medieval knight's quest. God erects signs along the way to guide us on our journey—godwinks to assure us that we are indeed on the right path.

As I take you into the journeys of those in the following stories, think about the desires that have been placed into your heart, signaling you toward your destiny. What have you done lately to move toward the realization of your dreams, to conquer your quests?

GOD WINKS ON QUESTS

BILLY'S WISHES AND WINKS

Billy Graham was only five years old, but he was excited by the man's words. From where he was sitting next to his father, he could see that other people were feeling it too. The passionate words of evangelist Billy Sunday filled the huge tent, and everybody was stirred.

As he grew up, Billy thought a lot about the power of words to arouse emotion.

When Billy was sixteen, the oratorical skills of evangelist Dr. Mordecai Fowler Ham grabbed his mind and gripped his heart, further fascinating him with some people's special abilities to captivate others with words.

Four years later as a student at the Florida Bible Institute in Tampa, Billy pursued his own emerging talents to preach—anywhere possible.

"I would paddle a canoe out to a little island where I could address all creatures great and small . . . from alligators to birds," he wrote in his autobiography, *Just As I Am*. And he was seen once sermonizing to a four-year-old boy seated atop a chest of drawers in the men's dormitory.

But the wish Billy held highest was the chance to preach at the West Tampa Gospel Mission in the city's Hispanic district.

He ruminated as to how he could possibly get an invitation to speak there. One day as he passed the mission, he decided to pray about it. He kneeled down on the lawn and prayed, right then and there.

Billy stood up moments later, startled that the kindly old man who ran the mission, whom everyone knew simply as Mr. Corwin, was approaching him.

"Billy," said Mr. Corwin, "our scheduled speaker for tomorrow had to cancel. Could you fill in for him?"

Absolutely astonished by such an immediate answer to his prayer, Billy could only nod. He could never have measured how pivotal that godwink was to become.

Billy's delivery was so impressive the next day that Mr. Corwin reissued the invitation for him to speak, many times over. And with that imprimatur came the confidence to take his preaching into the streets of Tampa. Six or seven times a day, every weekend, Billy would strengthen the power of his communication by preaching to whomever would gather. With every sermon, Billy honed his unique style.

After college Billy Graham took his ministry on the road. He would travel from town to town, preaching from temporary stages in tents to churches that offered pulpits. As he built his reputation one community at a time, national prominence seemed very distant.

One can never underestimate the power of godwinks . . . nor the force of a single little grandmother.

No one knows her name. She attended one of Billy Graham's revivals in a small town somewhere in America and was mesmerized by his unique abilities to articulate the English language. She thought everyone should know about him and decided to do something about it.

Picking up the phone, she dialed information and asked for the number for the home of Randolph Hearst, the newspaper magnate.

What are the chances that Randolph Hearst would answer the phone? He did. And in clear persuasive words, she told the world's most powerful publisher exactly how she felt about a young preacher named Billy Graham.

Hearst hung up the phone and directed his secretary to send a telegram to every one of his editors. It simply said, "Puff Graham."

Within days, newspaper readers across America were perusing stories about a dashing young preacher who was arresting audiences with his words. Within weeks, the name of Billy Graham was a household word.

Two small, turning-point godwinks—each beyond most people's comprehension—had propelled the career and quests of Billy Graham. A prayer instantaneously answered on a campus in Tampa, and the absurdly optimistic initiative of a lone woman who decided to telephone the most powerful communications man of the day.

During quiet, thoughtful times, Billy Graham has revisited in his mind each of these godwinks. Each time he says, "Thank you, Lord."

GETTING ON YOUR HIGHWAY

Billy Graham is widely respected. He has the unparalleled stature of being the only advisor to every president between Harry Truman and George W. Bush.

> Faith is the substance of things hoped for, the evidence of things not seen.
>
> —HEBREWS 11:1 NKJV

But the famous preacher would not have reached his destiny had he not gotten onto his universal highway—striking out in the direction he believed to be his destiny. And once he did, God put things in motion with that unbelievable godwink—a grandmotherly stranger placing an auspicious phone call.

Billy did not sit by the side of the road on his baggage, waiting for his destiny to come to him.

Nor should you.

Billy listened to the small voice within and made the choice to strike out, girded up by faith, in the direction he believed his destiny to be.

So must you.

Leave your baggage behind and get onto your life's path, on a quest for your destiny. Your destiny will not come to you. You need to go to it. And this I promise: the godwinks will be there to guide you.

:: :: ::

UNSEEN, UNKNOWN QUESTS

Sometimes you'll be going along in life minding your own business, and all of a sudden, God will grab you by the lapels, give you a wink, and blast you into a brand-new orbit. You find yourself soaring . . . dealing with an opportunity that hadn't crossed your mind, that you hadn't desired or even had known existed.

That's what happened in the next story. Sue Ellen Cooper was just shopping one day. That's all. And into an ordinary day came an extraordinary godwink that fostered radical change—for the better.

RED HAT POWER

Sue Ellen and her husband, Allen Cooper, were browsing through a thrift shop in downtown Tucson. It wasn't just a pastime. As an artist, Sue Ellen always scouted for small furniture items that she could paint with gaily-colored symbols, flowers, or birds, turning ordinary cabinets, chairs, or side tables into offbeat items for resale in a shop back in their hometown of Fullerton, California.

Passing an accessory counter, Sue Ellen stopped. She was drawn to a hat that somehow seemed to connect with her— to something somewhere deep in her memory.

It was a bold red hat.

Gently she raised the hat to her head, and with a slight lift of the chin and a sideways glance, she smiled approvingly into the mirror. Then with a tug of self-consciousness, she lifted a hand to remove it.

"Hey, that looks great!" said Allen, breaking into her reverie.

"Really?"

"It looks good."

"You think so? What would I do with it?"

"Well, just wear it tonight. It looks great on you," Allen encouraged.

She looked at the price on the inside of the brim. Printed in black felt-tip, it was $7.50.

Again she looked into the mirror, admiring the bright red hat, her mind again searching for the missing connection that eluded her.

"Okay," she acquiesced with a smile and a last glance in the mirror. "Yeah, I'll wear it. It'll be fun."

Shortly thereafter, her memory connected the dots to a red hat from her childhood. Ah . . . *that* was the attraction! As a child she had an imaginary playmate, a tiny woman who wore a red hat!

I can still see her as plain as day, thought Sue Ellen. *She wore a little red pancake hat with plastic cherries on it. My made-up name for her was Mrs. Silkens.*

Three months later, the red hat reentered Sue Ellen's mind. She'd been pondering a gift for her best friend Linda's fifty-fourth birthday.

If it had been anyone else, she wouldn't have thought of the gift she'd decided on.

She's not easy to buy for . . . not the traditional woman who loves another piece of jewelry or nightgown . . . I'll get her something special, something that makes her feel good about her age, she resolved.

Her mind drifted to a poem she'd read somewhere—

"Warning" by English poet Jenny Joseph—that went something like this:

> "When I am an old woman I shall wear purple,
> With a red hat which doesn't go and doesn't suit me."[1]

That's it! I'll get her a red hat like the one I found in Tucson, concluded Sue Ellen. *She can hang it on a wall along with a framed copy of that poem.*

On Sunday mornings before church, Linda, Sue Ellen, and their husbands customarily had breakfast at Polly's Pies in Fullerton.

"Happy Birthday to you," Sue Ellen half-spoke, half-sang as she handed Linda a gift bag.

"I love it, I love it," repeated Linda as she tried on her vintage red hat for all to see, right there in the café.

And that was just the beginning of the power of the red hat.

"The next thing you know, all our other friends thought it was neat. Our friend, Carol, was turning fifty the next month, so I gave her the second red hat. And because I wanted to take the fear out of turning that age, we decided you have to be fifty to wear a red hat. I was feeling what other women in my age group felt . . . like . . . 'Dang it. I'm not dead, and I'm not done.'

"And our friends all said, *Me too!*"

So Sue Ellen bought several more red hats and poems.

"The hats weren't easy to find," reminded Allen.

"That's right. And they weren't cheap. They were vintage, so you had to seek them out."

Six months after Linda received the first red hat for her birthday, Sue Ellen conjured up a fun idea.

"We're going to go to tea. And we're going to wear our red hats and purple dresses," she announced to her friends.

"We had so much fun that day," she recalled. "I think it was the dress-up thing that made it so special. And we got silly."

Someone said, "Sue Ellen, you're a queen for thinking of this."

"Yes. That's it! I'm the queen," she replied. "And we're going to be the Red Hat Society."

With that, Sue Ellen—the one who always has fun with words—began to pronounce titles for the others around the table. From then on, she was the Exalted Queen Mother, and Linda was the Esteemed Vice Mother.

Linda had such a good time at the Red Hat tea that she told a friend in Florida. Pretty soon they started a group of Red Hatters there.

At a Christmas party, Linda encountered the editor of *Romantic Homes* magazine who said, "I'd love to do a story about your group." And not long after that, a local paper, the

Orange County Register, thought the Red Hat Society would be a cute feature for the holidays. The Associated Press decided to pick up the story, and it ran across the country.

"You might want to put your e-mail in the story," the journalist said.

"Well, I don't use a computer. Besides, why would anyone want to talk to me?" asked Sue Ellen. "Oh well, just put my phone number in there."

"Oh no. Trust me. You don't want to do that," said the journalist.

Sue Ellen quickly called a friend, who told her how to set up an instant e-mail account.

At first she hated the computer. But she had to learn. She thought she could take an hour a day from her art to answer the e-mails that kept pouring in.

"We had maybe twenty e-mails a day, then it was fifty, and it just kept growing. Pretty soon, it was all I was really able to do."

"You have to have your own computer," counseled Allen. "I can't get my work done." He was then working for a medical company and was trying to complete a surgical manual.

"The e-mails would say, 'That sounds like fun, how can we start a Red Hat chapter?' They seemed to need permission or some direction," said Sue Ellen.

Soon the space at the house just wasn't enough. Sue Ellen

found a storage room for $200 a month, which served them for a few months. Then they had to move again, into a four-room office space; then later, to an even bigger place.

"It's been like that ever since," she reflected. "At each new point, I kind of think, *Well, that's probably about as far as this will go,* but when people ask me about the future, I just say, 'I haven't any more idea than you do.'"

Soon hundreds of people were asking how to start a chapter. For $35 per chapter, they could receive a kit in the mail with all the instructions.

"Women get together and just start giggling," said Sue Ellen. "Some of the chapter names are so clever—Grape Expectations, Raising Canes, the Boston Baked Beings. I love words . . . and they're having more fun than they ever did."

Why?

"They love the royalty. The play. The dress-up. Women get together and they sew matching pajamas for Red Hat pajama parties."

At some point, Sue Ellen and Allen decided they ought to have a convention. *But how do you go about doing that?* they wondered.

Their son-in-law, Matt Reekstin, reminded them that his father had experience planning meetings for his professional group . . . he knew about booking hotels and things of that sort.

Soon after, Sue Ellen ran into the owner of a shop that had sold her painted furniture. Sabrina Contreras and her sister, Debra Granich, were at the same gift show in Los Angeles as Sue Ellen was that day. (*There's* a godwink!) They were amazed to hear of the latest developments in the Red Hat Society. When Sue Ellen told them about the upcoming convention, they asked how she was handling it all. In the course of their conversation, it became evident that Sabrina, with experience in merchandising, and Debra, who had just left an executive position with the Disney Corporation, had skills that Sue Ellen and her husband were in dire need of. Within a very short time, they agreed to work together.

Not long after that, the first Red Hat Society convention unfolded at Chicago's Sheraton Hotel.

"We didn't know what the heck we were doing," said Sue Ellen.

"We had no idea," added Allen.

"I don't know how we pulled that off," said Sue Ellen.

"But it was that convention that really shook me up!" observed Allen. "It was 'splash me in the face with cold water'— I couldn't believe that four hundred people would show up."

A year later, they had another convention.

Two thousand women were there for that one in Nashville. There were hundreds more the next year in Dallas.

And just as I write this story, the Red Hat Society has had its fourth annual convention, filling two Las Vegas hotels, turning away registrants when they reached capacity: fifty-four hundred attendees!

Debra Granich's natural executive skills come into play, running the day-to-day activities, preparing Red Hatters for the ever-expanding national conventions, the several mini-conventions of fifteen hundred to two thousand attendees, and several expos around the country.

Sabrina Contreras manages the merchandising, is in charge of the Red Hat stores over the Web, and attends every convention.

Sue Ellen's and Allen's daughter, Andrea Reekstin, is in charge of creative development. Andrea's husband, Matt, helps with conventions and finances, in addition to his physical therapy business. Several other family members of the Cooper, Contreras, and Granich families also contribute time and effort to the Red Hat Society.

The joy that emanates from thousands of Red Hat attendees is truly inspiring. What started out as a lark—a fun idea to make her friends feel good about turning fifty—has become an enormous sisterhood for women who have reached a place where they feel that there's so much more to do . . . places to go . . . things to see.

The Red Hat Society is a blessing for those women whom

society has forgotten such as widows, who are left adrift by the loss of their husbands. While coping with the loss of their mate, the man of the house, the person who made them "a couple" . . . they, all too often, find themselves alone, sometimes "uninvited" to events by former friends because of an unstated fear that a widow might tempt the affections of married men.

The Red Hat Society offers women the chance to just get out and have fun with "the girls." Chapter after chapter form theater parties, cruises, teas, and other events. Best of all, they relish the stir they create when a half-a-dozen or a dozen Red Hatters—gaily decked out in red hats, boas, and purple attire—enter a restaurant.

The dress-up becomes a badge of honor . . . a uniform for frivolity. And observers quickly dub Red Hatters as fun-loving people.

As it has mushroomed, the Red Hat Society has become much more than fun. They now represent thousands of inspirational stories that have been published in Sue Ellen's books.

She tells of a woman she met in Michigan. Health problems besieged the woman for years, and another huge blow came when her doctor told her that unless she had a leg amputated, she would die.

She had decided to die.

Her dear Red Hat Society chapter friends rallied around

her and convinced her that whether she was ready to give up or not, *they* were not ready to lose *her*. Soon she had the surgery, and there she was . . . attending the Las Vegas convention, having the time of her life!

Another lady confided to Sue Ellen: "I hadn't laughed in two years. You see, I lost my twenty-seven-year-old son two years ago. If it weren't for the Red Hat Society, I'd be dead."

On the dance floor at Studio 54 in Vegas, a seventy-five-year-old woman shouted out, "Thank you, Sue Ellen! I feel like I'm sixteen again."

As an enormous chain reaction—not just across America, but across the world—the Red Hat Society, in only five years, has burst into a powerful force. They add an average of seventy-five new chapters every day, with memberships in multiple countries. As of this writing, Sue Ellen estimates that there are nearly one million members.

Sue Ellen and Allen are still baffled by it all.

"I feel like Forrest Gump when he started running," said Sue Ellen. "I think, *Where are we going?* . . . and as I keep running, they're right there behind me. I'm like, *Well, let's just see.*"

Every so often, Sue Ellen's mind goes back to that godwink moment . . . looking into a mirror in a Tucson thrift shop . . . admiring a red hat she'd just placed on her head . . . and the playful wink from God that reminded her of her imaginary childhood friend, Mrs. Silkens, who also wore a red hat.

And then there was Allen's comment: "You look great! You should wear it."

"What if I'd said nothing?" Allen now wonders.

What a wonderful godwink that he *did* speak up.

Think of all the Red Hatter joy that has transpired since.

There's a postscript to this story . . . for Sue Ellen *and* her imaginary friend of long ago. At a regional convention of Red Hatters in Boston, John Harney, founder of the Harney Tea Company, announced that he was producing a new brand: Red Hat Tea.

He told Sue Ellen that it was a state-of-the-art teabag. The new bag is part silk, part linen.

"We have a name for it," he said. "We call it Silk-en."

Sue Ellen stared at him, wondering, *Could he know? Of my friend Mrs. Silkens?*

No. Just another incredible godwink!

THE STORY OF THE STORY

Winding through traffic, Candy Chand glanced at her watch. Christmas was days away, and the stresses of the season were making her shoulders ache. Furrowing her brow, she mentally reviewed her list of to-dos. Was she mistaken, or was she adding more than subtracting?

The priority of the moment—get to Nicholas's school on time. His kindergarten class was having dress rehearsal for the so-called "winter pageant."

"Why don't they call it what it is?" she said out loud, to no one.

Her mind moved to a more harmonious thought: *Thank God Nicholas has no problem with my night schedule at the hospital.* It was a blessing that at five he was oblivious to his mommy's coming to dress rehearsal, rather than the real performance that evening.

"No prima donna there," she smiled. Nicholas was a no-stress kid. But the very mention of "stress" took her mind back to the earlier thought.

"Winter pageant? Don't get me started," she said, shaking her head in quick little movements, searching through the windshield, confirming that, again, none of the stores displayed the word *Christmas.*

Christ is rejected, and so am I, she thought.

How many publisher rejections do I now have for my children's book? She'd lost count. It was small comfort to have the nicest stack of turn-downs: "A fourth-grade girl's diary is a good idea

. . . but . . ." "Your children's book, *Nikki Lamar's Private Diary*, has compelling characters and dialogue . . . but . . ."

She was glad she'd accepted the bad news and stopped fighting it, learning from the cancer patients at the hospital that there is a comforting peace in accepting the inevitable. Sometimes acceptance of what *is*, is so much less stressful than fighting a fruitless battle.

She dreaded what her mother might think. Now in heaven, her mom had always said, "You're going to be a writer when you grow up, Candy."

Would she be disappointed?

Pulling into the school parking lot, Candy expelled a quiet sigh. Small miracle. She'd gotten there on time.

A few other parents and teachers were gathered in the cafeteria ready to witness the unfolding of this season's Christmas pageant. *There, I've said it,* she thought defiantly, repeating herself loudly, "*Christ-mas pageant!*"

How cute can kindergarteners be? she mused, an involuntary smile sweeping over her face as she watched the five-year-olds herded by their teacher into position for their big number.

As they began, Candy drew in a breath. She realized they were about to sing a song called "Christmas Love." Her appreciation for Nicholas's teacher and the school instantly soared. Imagine that! The selection of a song that used the actual word of the holiday being celebrated was bold and praiseworthy.

But Candy was totally unprepared for the godwink that followed.

As the adorable flock of children adorned in red and white scarves and fuzzy mittens commenced their performance, a godwink unfolded that became indelibly imprinted on her memory—and changed her life.

"I instantly knew that God was sending me a message," she reflected, "a clear sign that quitting my quest to write was not an option—and He was giving me the story right then and there."

> All will know that you are My disciples, if you have love for one another.
>
> —JOHN 13:35 NKJV

The heartwarming story, *Christmas Love*, that later poured out on Candy's computer screen was soon read around the globe, forwarded by one Internet user after another. She described the godwink this way:

The performance was going smoothly, until suddenly, we noticed her—a small quiet girl in the front row holding the letter "M" upside down—totally unaware her letter "M" appeared as a "W." The audience of first through sixth graders snickered at this little one's mistake. But she had no idea they were laughing at her, so she stood tall, proudly holding her "W." Although many teachers tried to shush the children, the laughter continued until the last letter was raised, and we all saw it together. A hush came over the audience and eyes began to widen. In that instant, we understood—the reason we were there, why we celebrated the holiday in the first place, why even in the chaos there was a purpose for our festivities. For when the last letter was held high, the message read loud and clear: CHRIST WAS LOVE. And I believe He still is.

Candy Chand's godwink was a nod from God to hang in there. Not to give up writing. Her story *Christmas Love* was subsequently published in *Chicken Soup for the Christian Family Soul,* and that paved the way for her to fulfill her mother's prophecy and the desires within her own heart. She's the author of four books. Her fifth, *The Twelve Prayers of Christmas,* is due out soon.

DON KNOTTS'S BIG DAY

Many would agree that television's most enduring, most likeable character is Barney Fife from *The Andy Griffith Show.* As the deputy sheriff with an empty gun, Barney was the quintessential sidekick. He could make you laugh just by pursing his lips, wearing a surprised look, and nervously shaking his head. We came to know him synonymously with the actor who played him, Don Knotts.

Don Knotts was a struggling New York actor in the mid-'50s. Like many others in his shoes, he would hang out at the NBC drugstore, hoping that some good fortune—or at the very least, some useful casting gossip—would come his way.

Late one afternoon, he shared a cup of coffee with an acquaintance—another wannabe actor who had a tidbit of hot information. That day a downtown casting agent was holding final auditions for a new Broadway play.

Don looked at the clock. It was almost 4:30. He calculated that if he rushed to the subway, he might make it there before five.

Soon Don was dashing through throngs of people on New York streets, bounding down the subway steps two at a time, and jostling through the crowds to get alongside the subway. He anxiously looked at his watch. The train was late. Finally it came.

At Wall Street he bolted through masses of people, up the stairs to the street. He quickly looked around to get his bearings. Then he saw the casting agent's address, right across the street. Taking a chance he dashed through midblock traffic into the building, scanned the directory in the entry, and quickly leaped up the stairs to the second floor offices.

Out of breath, Don encountered an officious assistant sitting at a desk. The man didn't look at all happy that Don had arrived at the last minute.

"I . . . I came for the auditions," gasped Don, out of breath.

"Finished," clipped the dour assistant.

Don Knotts looked at him. Pursing his lips like Barney Fife would do years later—with a surprised wide-eyed look and a slight shaking of the head—he said: "Finished? You mean I rushed all the way down here just to find the auditions are all over?"

The assistant nodded.

Don hung his head, slowly turned, slumped out of the offices, down the stairs, and across the street to the subway for a disappointing ride back to midtown.

He was about to take a step that would have hidden him from ground-level view when his ear caught a voice breaking through the din of New York street traffic.

"*Wait!*"

He stopped.

"Wait!" the voice repeated.

Don turned to see the casting agent's assistant hanging out the second floor window across the street.

Secure he'd caught Don's attention, the casting agent was

motioning him back.

Puzzled, Don reascended the steps to the second floor office.

With the smile of a sycophant, the assistant explained in a conspiratorial whisper: "You looked so sad, I told the boss he just had to see you."

Don was given a few pages of script from the new play *No Time for Sergeants* and asked to read for the casting agent.

Within a few days he was leaping with the kind of joy that a struggling actor experiences when he finally gets a break. He had landed a small role in what was to become a hit Broadway show, created especially for another promising new actor.

But more important, the godwink that occurred when the casting agent's assistant prevailed upon his boss to see just one more actor—and the good fortune of his capturing Don Knotts's attention just before he submerged into the subway—was one of the most auspicious events in Don's life because the promising new actor he was to play against was Andy Griffith.

That pairing of personalities developed the successful comedy relationship that later became perfect casting for *The Andy Griffith Show.*

Paths Will Change

You'll be astounded by the number of times that your course will be corrected by a divine navigational system, as you strike out putting yourself in motion toward what you believe to be your destiny. You may think a path is leading you toward your quest, but then you "just happen" to bump into someone who moves you into a whole new direction. Someone you fall in love with. Someone who causes you to change your geographical location. Or someone like Don Knotts's friend, who led him to a job opportunity that placed him in a Broadway play that affected the trajectory of the rest of his life.

> It is never too late to be what you might have been.[2]
> —GEORGE ELIOT

As I've mentioned before, these unwitting messengers of goodness are Godwink Links—people like you and me, whom God uses to deliver winks of assurance to others and to alter their paths.

This is certain: Your direction toward your destiny will never be altered, and your course will never be corrected if you are still sitting by the side of the road. You must stay in motion—and stay alert for God's winks.

THE QUEST OF THE HAUNTING PHOTO

Rich Luttrell stood before the Wall in Washington, DC, a

black wall of granite incised with names of the service people who died in the Vietnam conflict.

It's a somber place. War is not glorified at this memorial. Instead, visitors are moved to tears by the unlived lives—and living heartaches—represented by the fifty-eight thousand names on the Wall.

Lips move silently, tears drop, an object is set down—a hat, a mess kit, a can of beer, a teddy bear, a baby's pacifier, a watch, a folded American flag. Others watch in silent compassion.

Would it change things? Coming here, leaving a bit of grief at the Wall?

Rich, a vet from the Midwest, hoped it would. As his hand slipped into his pocket to complete his mission, his mind flashed to a scene imbedded in his memory, twenty-two years earlier.

The year was 1967.

It was a suffocating day in Chu Lai, Vietnam—the stifling heat and still air were held captive under steam-smudged skies.

Rich Luttrell had not yet seen the enemy. He hoped he wouldn't. He didn't want to fight anyone in these conditions— picking his way over rotted stumps, tangled vines, and mud potholes on a jungle trail.

An imposing question pressed against his mind. Who might be lurking behind those leaves, trees, and vines, waiting to ambush him?

That day was no different than others . . . the heat, the mud, the fear, the exhaustion.

Not until one flash of movement changed everything.

Instinctively, Rich swung to face the movement, his rifle raised, every nerve ending standing at alert. Through his cross-hairs, a youthful NVA soldier was pointing an AK-47 at his head.

Momentarily they were alone. No one else was visible.

Standing in the jungle, guns aimed at each other, they could have been the last two men on earth.

It was the longest one second in Rich's life.

Why didn't the man shoot? He had the element of surprise.

For a hanging second, their eyes locked. Somewhere inside, two souls seemed to seek compromise in an impossible situation.

In the second that only oozed forward, Rich the soldier was called to follow orders.

Bam!

His gun exploded.

Bam! The enemy's gun fired.

Bam . . . bam! Before he could think, Rich fired at two other NVAs who stepped from the brush.

Suddenly, there was a heavy firefight . . . other soldiers, friendly and unfriendly, were firing weapons.

Moments after it began, it was over.

The squad of North Vietnamese soldiers pulled back, disappearing into the brush.

Rich had won a battle. The evidence was at his feet—three corpses. But the teenager from Illinois had lost something that day that he would never find again. He lost his innocence. Somehow he'd never made it to a school prom, but on that day against his own wishes, he'd become a warrior.

Someone approached the first dead man and pulled a wallet from his uniform. Rich caught sight of something fluttering to the ground. He picked it up and looked at it—a photo. Rich looked down at the man for a long moment, looked back at the photo, and quietly slipped it into his own pocket.

Something unstated had passed between them.

Now forty-year-old Rich Luttrell stood at the Wall. Since that day in Chu Lai long ago, he had become a husband, a father of girls, and a loyal employee of the state government of Illinois.

All in all, it had been a good life, except for that one grief that hovered, sometimes landed and stayed. He traveled to the Wall in hopes that he could end the vigil he'd kept. Praying his grief would find closure.

As his wife watched, he pulled two items from his pocket, a tiny tattered photograph and a letter he handwrote the night before.

No bigger than a postage stamp, the photo showed a handsome, unsmiling Vietnamese father in his late twenties with a slight frown drawing his eyebrows together. He was wearing his green NVA uniform. Next to him was a beautiful girl about seven years old with meticulously groomed, braided pigtails. She was not smiling either.

All those years, the photograph was as precious to Rich as photos of his own daughters. He had carried it in his wallet since the day he picked it up from the dead soldier.

Sometimes his daughters would give him a new wallet for Christmas. With each new wallet, the old wallet's contents were removed, the photo brought out, gazed at, and then carefully placed in the new wallet. With each new wallet and each fresh examination of the photo came a crushing sadness.

"There's a young girl who doesn't have a father, thanks to me," he'd remark to himself.

"Why don't you get rid of it?" his wife asked so many times over the years, sensing the depression that enveloped Rich as he mentally returned to that jungle in Chu Lai.

As time passed, the photo became far more than a memento. The dead man earned his respect—even his devotion, in an odd sort of way. The child engendered a sacred trust. He didn't know why, what the trust was, or what he should do with it. But he just wasn't able to get rid of it.

The soldier and his daughter deserved more. The photograph deserved more. It finally became clear to him.

What more appropriate place to lay down the photo—and hopefully his guilt—than at the Vietnam Veterans Memorial?

The night before, Rich penned a personal message to the soldier whose life he had taken—to the father of the daughter he had orphaned:

Dear Sir,

For twenty-two years, I have carried your picture in my wallet. I was only eighteen years old that day we faced one another on that trail in Chu Lai, Vietnam. Why you did not take my life I'll never know. You stared at me for so long, armed with your AK-47, and yet you did not fire. Forgive me for taking your life, I was reacting just the way I was trained, to kill V. C. or gooks. Hell, you weren't even considered human.

So many times over the years, I have stared at your picture of you with your daughter, I suspect. Each time my heart and guts would burn with the pain of guilt. I have two daughters myself now.

Today, I visit the Vietnam Veterans Memorial in D.C. I have wanted to come here for several years now to say goodbye to many of my former comrades.

I truly loved many of them, as I am sure you loved many

of your former comrades.

As of today, we are no longer enemies. I perceive you as a brave soldier defending his homeland. Above all else, I can now respect the importance that life held for you. I suppose that is why I am able to be here today. It is time for me to continue the life process and relieve my pain and guilt.

As I leave here today, I leave your picture and this letter. Forgive me, Sir, I shall try to live my life to the fullest, an opportunity that you and many others were denied.

So until we chance to meet again in another time and place, rest in peace.

Respectfully,

Richard A. Luttrell

101st Airborne Division

Rich stepped forward, stooped, and set the photograph and letter against the Wall.

He remembered how he felt: "It was a way to honor and respect him. It was like saying good-bye to a friend. At that moment, it was like I had just finished a firefight and dropped my rucksack and got to rest. That load I was carrying was gone."

Rich walked away, after paying respects to buddies whose names were etched there. The past was finally behind him.

"I felt free, I felt relieved," he said.

The photo was about to live on, even out of Rich's hands, with a power of its own.

Objects left at the Wall are picked up twice a day by gloved National Park Service rangers, tagged with a reference number, the date, and location where it was left. Thousands of objects are retrieved each year and shipped to the National Park Service Museum Resource Center (MRCE) in Landover, Maryland, where more than fifty thousand items will never again see the light of day.

Just one of a score of objects picked up that day, Rich's photo and letter were recorded and laid in a box.

A godwink—they landed at the top of the box. Face up.

Duery Felton, Jr. learned the suffering in Vietnam firsthand. He had not seen the green NVA uniform in thirty years. Nor had he wanted to. His time in Vietnam was the worst that life could deliver. It was locked away in some part of his mind. He wouldn't speak about it.

As curator of the Vietnam Veterans Memorial Collection, he felt he was chosen by providence for the sacred job of caretaking the memories of nine million Vietnam-era veterans. He considered himself a conduit to their history.

He counseled his employees—Vietnam veterans all—to

try to maintain an emotional distance from the objects they handled.

"If you were to read all this and take it inside yourself, you would lose your mind. One guy's combat diary . . . I had to walk out the door that day," said Duery, shaking his head sadly.

Staring up at him from the top of a box of artifacts was the most unsettling of images: the small photo of an NVA soldier and a girl. In several years on the job, that was the first time anyone had ever left a photo of an enemy soldier. He felt a choking nausea as he looked at it. But as he read Rich's letter, his tension eased . . . he felt a release. Someone had put down on paper the swirl of anguished emotions about Vietnam's legacy that were the same as his.

Duery respectfully lifted the photo and letter from the box.

In the coming months, in talks and exhibits about the Wall, he used the letter and photo to help people understand the lingering effects of war on its soldiers.

And now, the lingering effects of the photo were passed from Rich Luttrell to a new bearer.

"It haunted me for years and years, as to who the little girl was," Duery said.

In the early 1990s, Turner Publishing asked Duery to help create a book about artifacts left at the Vietnam Memorial. Among Duery's first choices for inclusion in the book *Offerings at the Wall,* released in 1995, were the photo and letter.

Rich Luttrell knew none of this.

In the six years since Rich had left the photo at the wall, his life had been blessed; he had two daughters and two small granddaughters to love.

One morning in 1996, his peace was shattered when Ron Stephens, an Illinois state congressman and a decorated veteran of Vietnam, burst into a meeting in Rich's office. Someone had given Ron a copy of *Offerings at the Wall.* Casually leafing through the pages, his jaw dropped. What he saw pulled him to his knees. He knew the photo; he knew who wrote the letter. His friend, Rich Luttrell, had once shared with him the story of his grief and how he had found solace by leaving the photo and a letter in Washington, DC.

"You got a minute?" Ron asked as he nodded to the others in the meeting.

Rich's face clouded as he saw the title of the book.

When Ron opened it to page fifty-three, Rich stared.

And wept.

"Little girl, what do you want from me?" he choked.

From that moment, Rich's life turned nightmarish. His obsession returned—stronger than before.

Now he knew what he had to do.

But first he had to get the picture back.

He tracked down Duery at the Vietnam Veterans Memorial Collection and asked that the photo be returned to him. Although it was contrary to policy to return artifacts left at the Wall, Duery made an exception. The photo had a life force that could not be denied. He flew to Illinois to personally deliver it to Rich.

With the photo back in hand, Rich's quest began.

The photo cycled through many lives and came back to him for a reason. Twenty-two years in his wallet, four or five years working its way through the heart of another vet, finding its way into a book, and now—back into his hands.

He had succeeded in releasing his guilt, but now he felt an unfulfilled obligation: To find the little girl—to give her the picture of her father. And to tell her that her father died nobly, with concern for an enemy soldier.

"That little girl won't leave me alone. If that's the way she wants it, I guess I'm just going to have to find her," vowed Rich.

He began by contacting a newspaper reporter in St. Louis. When the story of his quest was in print, he folded up the paper and dispatched it to the Vietnamese ambassador in Washington, DC, asking him for his help in finding the girl.

The ambassador sent the story on to someone he knew in Hanoi, knowing it would be a tall order. Literally, a needle in a haystack.

With eighty million people in Vietnam, many of whom were beyond the reach of the media, finding the child in the photo would be a miracle. She would be in her late forties if she were even alive. What were the chances that anyone would recognize her, or a man who'd been dead for thirty years?

In Hanoi a local newspaper reporter, fascinated by the photo and letter, published it under the heading "Does anyone know these people?"

Not surprisingly, in a city of three million, no one did.

Nor was Rich surprised. "I didn't really expect anything to come out of it," he said, "but it was something I had to do, to give it a shot."

Again, he felt some peace. After all, he had done everything he could.

The Bible counsels, "Having done all . . . stand."[3] Yet often at the very moment a person has done everything he can, and he truly *stands*—turning the matter over to the Almighty— that's when God will wink.

A woman in a rural Vietnamese village opened a package from her son in Hanoi. Her gift was cushioned in crumbled newspaper. As she began to discard the old newspaper wrappings, she suddenly stopped—dumbfounded. Her eyes gazed upon something too precious for words: the image of her dead brother and his child!

This godwink was a gift far more precious to her than even the care package from her beloved son.

"Does anyone know these people?" asked the newspaper.

In a country of eighty million, one person did.

She got up and began walking. Her dead brother's daughter lived down the road.

In Springfield, Illinois, Rich Luttrell walked to his mailbox. It was the translation he'd been waiting for of a strange letter that had arrived earlier, handwritten in Vietnamese.

Is this it? he wondered, tremulously holding the translated letter. What possible hurt, anger, or sadness—or all three—might it contain?

He was awash with emotions.

The letter was from the girl in the picture!

Now a grown-up woman named Lan, she wrote in almost childlike sweetness:

Dear Mr. Richard,

   The child that you have taken care of, through the picture, for over thirty years, she becomes adult now, and she had spent so much sufferance in her childhood by the missing of her father.

   I hope you will bring the joy and happiness to my family.

Rich shook his head in disbelief.

He reread the words "I hope you will bring the joy and happiness to my family." She was offering a gift of her forgiveness. She wanted to see him.

But how could he go back to Vietnam and face a woman whom he had left fatherless? Rich had no regrets over his actions as a soldier; but the *effects* of those actions seemed to be almost unforgivable, even to him.

Why go back and reopen old wounds?

Rich and Lan traded letters and photos over the next several months. She invited him to turn his grief and haunting into joy and happiness. He was astounded at her generous spirit.

This whole thing's bigger than I am. It's hard for me to understand, but I know this is the right thing to do, he said to himself.

He began his journey back to Vietnam.

Eight thousand miles later, in a distant Vietnamese village, Rich began walking toward a house behind a brick wall. Lan and her family were gathered in the courtyard on the other side, waiting for him. She stood slightly apart from the rest.

Lan was unsmiling, giving no clue to her emotions. He walked to her, handed her a bouquet of flowers he'd brought with him, and in carefully practiced Vietnamese, said:

"Today, I return the photo of you and your father, which I have kept for thirty-three years."

He paused, swallowed.

"Please forgive me."

With that, he relinquished the photo into Lan's hands and ended a chapter that began in fear and violence three decades before.

Lan pressed her father's image to her forehead and collapsed sobbing into Rich's arms. The photo was between them—just as it had always been. It was now a bridge to peace.

After a torrent of tears, the two emerged from their embrace. Lan stared at the photo. She told Rich it was the only picture she had of her father.

Rich told Lan and her family, who were hungry for information about Lan's father: "Your father died a brave and courageous warrior."

Hugging Rich again, Lan said she believed he brought her father's spirit home to her family, her brother, and her.

They believed their father lived on in Rich.

They forgave Rich.

No Odds with God

Rich Luttrell had a quest much bigger than most of ours. It had impossible odds of success. He learned, as you and I need to remind ourselves, that with God there are no odds. Nothing is impossible.

Still, it is incredible how He worked so many godwinks into Rich's story. How in the act of war, a symbol of life, a tiny personal photograph, fell from a dead man's wallet; how that photo seemed to possess Rich for twenty-two years until he left it among hundreds of artifacts at the Wall in D.C. How the photograph and Rich's personal letter ended up on the *top* of the box of artifacts and moved the spirit of another veteran, who in turn, used the photo and letter to teach others about the toll of war—in his lectures and in a book.

> You are a God of forgiveness, gracious and merciful . . . full of unfailing love and mercy.
>
> —NEHEMIAH 9:17 NLT

Finally, the extraordinary godwink that the photo was published, and that it would end up in the Hanoi newspaper crumpled in a care package to a remote village in Vietnam, to be opened by the aunt of the girl who was sought by Rich Luttrell, eight thousand miles away.

This chain of godwinks that showered peace and forgiveness on two families on opposite sides of the globe is a remarkable tribute to God's power in each of our lives and how He places signposts of reassurance along the paths of each of our quests.

The Clarity of Quests

Often as you are on your journey toward your quests, you visualize the finish line; in your mind's eye you can see yourself enjoying the prize that has been the object of the desires of your heart—still, you remain unclear as to exactly how you are going to get there.

A mountain climber visualizes reaching the summit and has a plan to get there. He knows that many adjustments along the way will need to be made to correct his course. Moreover, the climber knows that if he sits at the bottom, waiting for the summit to come to him, it never will. He must get started, heading in the direction he believes to be the correct one. One toehold at a time.

Each of the people in this chapter, Billy Graham, Sue Ellen Cooper, Candy Chand, Don Knotts, and Rich Luttrell, all had desires placed in their hearts. Not until they put their hands on the steering wheels of their lives, and struck out toward their purpose, did extraordinary godwinks begin to unfold.

That is what will happen for you. And the closer you get to your summit, the clearer it will be.

CONCLUSION

One of the things I like the most about godwinks is that they are tangible signposts from God, making His presence known in our lives every single day.

If you want to be certain that God has been in your life all along, take the time to excavate your past, to uncover prior winks from God that you didn't notice, shrugged off, or forgot about. I recommend a mapping expedition of yourself.

MAPPING

Go back to those times in your life when you came to a crossroad. Your life changed abruptly. You lost someone you loved. You found a soul mate. You had a new baby. You moved geographically. You ran into someone that completely changed your career—or your belief system.

Revisit each of those times in your past to uncover godwinks that were sent to you even if you weren't paying attention. Make a list of the "coincidences" and answered prayers.

> I will use stories to speak my message and to explain things that have been hidden since the creation of the world.
>
> —MATTHEW 13:35 CEV

This is what you'll discover: when there were multiple paths that your life could've followed, there were always signposts of reassurance—godwinks of personal communication—to you and to no one else on Earth.

Here's more good news! The map of winks from God will continue to unfold long into your future. Just look for them. And acknowledge that He is communicating directly with you.

ACKNOWLEDGMENTS

Please join me in thanking some wonderful beings who made this book possible: my resolute literary agents Jan Miller and Michael Broussard; Paula Major, a marvelous editor; Nelson Books executives Jonathan Merkh and Greg Stielstra; and such key supporters as Heather Adams, Curt Harding, and Brandi Lewis. Almost most important . . . my support system in life . . . my lovely wife, Louise DuArt. And most important, God. He wrote it. I wrote it down.

NOTES

Chapter One: Godwinks Are Personal

"When It's Crystal Clear" is based on an anecdotal account given by Crystal
    Cathedral Sr. Pastor, Dr. Robert Schuller. Names are fictitious.

1. Nancy Gibbs, http://www.worldofquotes.com/author/Nancy-Gibbs/1/index.html,
    accessed 16 February 2006.

Chapter Two: Winks of Hope & Reassurance

1. Martin Buber, http://www.brainyquote.com/quotes/quotes/m/martinbube
    133855.html, accessed 16 February 2006.
2. Norman Vincent Peale, Sermon (preached 15 January 1967), Vol. 18, #17
    (Pawling, NY: Peale Center for Christian Living), 1967.
3. Helen Keller, http://www.brainyquote.com/quotes/authors/h/helen_keller.html,
    accessed 15 February 2006.
4. Tom Clancy, http://www.brainyquote.com/quotes/authors/t/tom_clancy.html,
    accessed 15 February 2006.

Chapter Three: God Winks on Transitions

"A Yellow Sea of Taxis" is reconstructed from TV interviews and "Aha! Moment,"
    O, The Oprah Magazine, October 2003.

1. John 3:36 NCV.
2. Kenneth Gamble and Leon Huff, "If You Don't Know Me by Now." Copyright
    1972. Warner-Tamerlane Publishing. All rights reserved. International copyright
    secured. Used by permission.
3. Civilla D. Martin (1866–1948), lyrics, and Charles H. Gabriel (1856–1932),
    music, "His Eye Is on the Sparrow," 1905.

Chapter Four: God Winks on Comfort

1. Jean Kerr, http://www.brainyquote.com/quotes/authors/j/jean_kerr.html,
    accessed 15 February 2006.

Chapter Five: God Winks on Prayer

"A Wink in Wichita" is from the original account told to the author via e-mail,
    June 2002. Names are fictitious.

"A Prayer of Reunion" is reconstructed from original accounts in newspaper and Internet stories, Associated Press, 25 December 2003. Names are fictitious.

1. "Use of Prayer or Noetic Therapy May Contribute to Better Outcomes in Cardiac Patients" (news release), 09 November 1998, Duke University Medical Center, http://www.dukemednews.org/news/article.php?id=486#top; "Prayer and Healing" (audio/video news), 20 November 2001, Duke University Medical Center, http://www.dukemednews.org/av/medminute.php?id=5136.

2. Kathleen Fackelmann, "The Power of Prayer: Six-Year Study Suggests People Can Be Blessed with Longer Lives," *USA Today*, McLean, VA, 18 July 2000.

3. Randolph C. Byrd, "Positive Therapeutic Effects of Intercessory Prayer in a Coronary Care Unit Population," *Southern Medical Journal*, Vol. 81, No. 7, July 1988, http://www.godandscience.org/apologetics/smj.pdf.

4. Harold G. Koenig, David B. Larson, Michael E. McCullough, *Handbook of Religion and Health* (New York: Oxford University Press, January 2001).

5. Fackelmann, Ibid.

6. Norman Vincent Peale, *The Power of Positive Thinking* (Englewood Cliffs, NJ: Prentice-Hall, 1952), 85.

7. John Updike, http://www.brainyquote.com/quotes/authors/j/john_updike.html, accessed 15 February 2006.

8. Peale, Ibid, 30.

9. Ol' Buffalo Favorite Quotes, "Duty to God," http://www.three-peaks.net/quotes.htm#god, accessed 27 March 2006.

Chapter Six: Winks on Unanswered Prayer

"Why Me? Why Now?" is reconstructed from TV and newspaper accounts, including CNN's *People in the News* and *The Oprah Winfrey Show*, regarding Mayor Rudolph Giuliani, 2001.

"The Smartest Mistake" is reconstructed from materials from Ruth's Chris Steak House corporate documents.

1. Patrick J. Alger, Larry Bastian, Garth Brooks, "Unanswered Prayers." Copyright 1990, Bait and Beer Music, Forerunner Music, Inc., Major Bob Music Company, Inc., and Mid-Summer Music, Inc. All rights reserved. International copyright secured. Used by permission.

2. Mark Twain, http://www.brainyquote.com/quotes/authors/m/mark_twain.html, accessed 15 February 2006.

3. Dolly Parton, http://www.brainyquote.com/quotes/authors/d/dolly_parton.html, accessed 15 February 2006.

4. John Wooden, http://www.brainyquote.com/quotes/authors/j/john_wooden.html, accessed 15 February 2006.

Chapter Seven: God Winks Just in Time

"Whew!" is the original account told to the author via e-mail, 18 August 2001. Names are fictitious.

"Morning Sounds" is based on Dr. Arnold Hutschnecker's personal account, related before his death to the author in 1997.

"The Giver of a Gift" is based on an original story e-mailed to the author. Names are fictitious.

1. Richard Bach, http://www.brainyquote.com/quotes/authors/r/richard_bach.html, accesses 15 February 2006.
2. Ralph Waldo Emerson, http://www.brainyquote.com/quotes/authors/r/ralph_waldo_emerson.html, accessed 15 February 2006.
3. Bob Carlisle and Randy Thomas, "Father's Love." Copyright 1999. All rights reserved. International copyright secured. Used by permission.
4. Ibid.

Chapter Eight: God Winks on Family

"Unlucky Day No More" is used by permission of terrywallisfund@hotmail.com.

"Brothers Waffle" is based on a personal story related to the author. Names are fictitious.

1. Theodore Isaac Rubin, MD, http://www.brainyquote.com/quotes/authors/t/theodore_isaac_rubin.html, accessed 15 February 2006.

Chapter Nine: God Winks on Quests

"Billy's Wishes & Winks" is reconstructed from various anecdotal accounts and Billy Graham's autobiography, *Just As I Am*, (HarperSanFrancisco/Zondervan, 1997).

1. Jenny Joseph, "Warning," http://www.brainyquote.com/quotes/authors/j/jenny_joseph.html, accessed 15 February 2006.
2. George Eliot, http://www.brainyquote.com/quotes/authors/g/george_eliot.html, accessed 15 February 2006.
3. Ephesians 6:13 NKJV.

About the Author

SQuire Rushnell, a former television president and CEO, was an executive with the ABC Television Network for twenty years. He was a creator of such programs for young people as *Schoolhouse Rock* and the ABC Afterschool Specials, which together won seventy-five Emmys. He also led *Good Morning America* to the number-one spot and is the author of the word-of-mouth phenomenon *When God Winks*.

 SQuire and his wife, entertainer and talk show host Louise DuArt, are the authors of *Couples Who Pray*. In this book, they take readers step by step through The 40 Day Prayer Challenge™ in which couples commit to praying together five minutes a day for forty days. Backed by compelling research and true-life experiences of 24 test couples including Denzel and Pauletta Washington, Kathie Lee and Frank Gifford, Donna Summer and Bruce Sudano, and Scott and Tracie Hamilton, SQuire and Louise reveal that daily prayer is a "life changing experience" in which most couples report positive outcomes in less than two weeks.